# Isabella's Journey

*Her battle with the blood disorder, Thalassemia Major.*

by Serafina Sammarco

# Isabella's Journey

*Her battle with the blood disorder, Thalassemia Major*

# Isabella's Journey

*Her battle with the blood disorder, Thalassemia Major*

Serafina Sammarco

ISBN (Paperback): 978-1-963565-43-0
ISBN (eBook): 978-1-963565-74-4

Library of Congress Control Number: 2024918450

Printed in the United States of America

Published by:

info@thequippyquill.com
(302) 295-2278

*To the memory of my daughter, Isabella Marie Sammarco*

# Table of Contents

Introduction ................................................................................. 1

## Chapter One

*Thalassemia: The Hard Fact* ............................................... 3

## Chapter Two

*My Roots and My Country* .................................................. 9

## Chapter Three

*Getting Married and Growing Up Fast* ........................... 13

## Chapter Four

*Isabella's Diagnosis* ........................................................... 19

## Chapter Five

*The Hospital; Our Second Home* ..................................... 23

## Chapter Six

*Vancouver, Here We Come* ............................................... 29

## Chapter Seven

*The Question* ....................................................................... 35

## Chapter Eight

*Tea Time and Desferal – Our Rituals* ............................. 41

## Chapter Nine

*Lending a Helping Hand*................................................................51

## Chapter Ten

*Growth Hormone Therapy* .............................................................55

## Chapter Eleven

*Japan and Hawaii* .........................................................................59

## Chapter Twelve

*Unscheduled Hospital Visit*...........................................................61

## Chapter Thirteen

*Preparing for the Inevitable*..........................................................69

## Chapter Fourteen

*Special Visitors* .............................................................................75

## Chapter Fifteen

*Our Last Farewell* .........................................................................79

## Chapter Sixteen

*The Grieving Process*......................................................................83

## Chapter Seventeen

*Forming a Support Group*..............................................................87

**Chapter Eighteen**

*Continuing On*....................................................................*91*

**Chapter Nineteen**

*My Thoughts on Thalassemia* ........................................*95*

Poems .................................................................................. 97

Acknowledgments............................................................ 105

Foundations and Resources ........................................... 107

About the Author ............................................................. 117

# Introduction

The main purpose of this book is to provide some insight into the genetic blood disorder thalassemia and the ripple effects that it has on patients and their families.

I truly hope that this book will inspire and give hope to the many sufferers of poor health. I attempt to explain thalassemia in simple layman's terms and in no way claim to be a medical expert.

Even though it has been a very difficult journey filled with obstacles to overcome, even after Isabella's death, we who have been left behind continue to live productive and joyous lives. I'm here to say that it is possible to be faced with tragedy and not only survive it but learn to appreciate life with all its wonders.

Thalassemia is not very well known or talked about by the media and the general public, although medical professionals are much more aware of it now than they were at the time of Isabella's diagnosis.

Everyone's personal voyage is unique, but it seemed to me that my daughter's journey was more challenging than most. The feelings of isolation and misunderstanding about thalassemia were not eased by the medical professionals who lacked the expertise to deal with this condition and its effects on the patient and the family.

My dream, as unrealistic as it may seem, is that one day thalassemia may be totally eradicated. My other goal is to provide some hope and inspiration to those families who are currently dealing with thalassemia. I want to ensure access to all of the available resources and, most importantly, quality health care for all thalassemia patients.

I decided to start the Vancouver Thalassemia Society just a few months after Isabella died because I needed to continue the legacy that she had started with her willingness to help others. The birth of this nonprofit society, which started as an informal support group, was made possible with the help and dedication of numerous individuals who worked long hours with me to make it all come together.

My burning desire to write a book and make a difference goes back many years, but for a long time I felt too numb to do anything other than the everyday essential chores and activities. I shelved this book project for many years and tried a variety of other things like volunteering, studying and learning new things and pursuing a career.

But the idea of writing Isabella's story kept coming back to me. So more than two decades after her death, I gave in to the urge that refused to go away.

# Chapter One

*Thalassemia: The Hard Fact*

My daughter was diagnosed with thalassemia major at the early age of eight months. Because my son, Peter, was a toddler only two years older than Isabella, I was suddenly overwhelmed by the responsibilities of being a new mom and caring for a child with grave medical needs. Neither my husband nor I had ever heard of this illness before.

I was only twenty-three years old, and Pasquale (Pat) was twenty-seven. Although we were both young, we took our responsibilities as parents seriously, and we were very much in love. We had a strong bond from the very beginning, which would carry us through the difficult times ahead.

There are many reasons why I want to tell Isabella's story, but two most important ones come to mind. One is to educate and provide some information on what thalassemia is and how deeply it affects the entire family. The second is that although this has been, without a doubt, a very difficult journey for our immediate and extended family and friends, I wanted to write about how this experience has also enriched and touched our lives in a very profound way.

Thalassemia is a virtually unknown blood disorder, yet it affects so many people all over the world, either directly or indirectly. I say "directly or indirectly" because there is more than one kind of thalassemia.

Thalassemia is a severe and particular form of anemia in which the body does not produce enough healthy red blood cells. It is these cells that carry oxygen from the lungs to all parts of the body.

Therefore, a shortage of these cells means that the body is deprived of oxygen.

The severity of the disease can vary from one individual to another, depending on a number of factors.

In thalassemia minor, an individual is only a carrier of the gene and can lead a normal, productive, and healthy long life; no transfusions are necessary. With thalassemia intermediate, a carrier may need a transfusion from time to time. This can be difficult because there is no established routine on how often a carrier should receive blood transfusions. When thalassemia major occurs an individual has inherited the thalassemia gene from both parents; therefore, the body does not produce enough red blood cells to survive and consequently will need regular blood transfusions.

There is a theory that because the thalassemia trait has some resistance to malaria, the disease has evolved in regions where malaria is prevalent.

Thalassemia is a genetic blood disorder, meaning it is an inherited condition present from the moment of conception. It cannot be caught from another child, nor can it develop later in life. The disease is passed on through parents who both carry the thalassemia gene in their own cells.

Pat and I are of Italian origin, and Isabella inherited the beta type of the disorder that is more prevalent among people of this origin. When both parents are carriers of the thalassemia gene, there is a one in four chance (25 percent) with each pregnancy that the child will inherit the thalassemia gene from both parents and therefore have the disorder called beta thalassemia major. There is a two in four chance (50 percent) chance with each pregnancy that the child will inherit the thalassemia gene from only one parent and a normal gene from the other and therefore be an unaffected carrier like the parents. There is just one chance in four (25 percent) with each pregnancy that the child will inherit normal genes from both parents and therefore be completely unaffected.

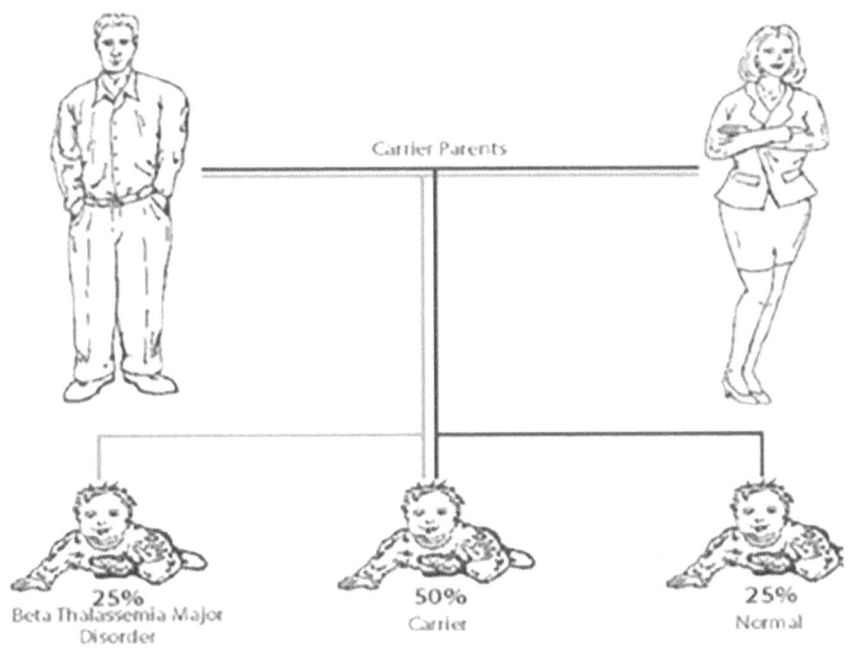

*This drawing illustrates the effect on a child when both parents are carriers of the thalassemia gene, as well as the chances of passing it on. Drawing by Andrea Autelitano*

Most children with thalassemia seem healthy for the first few months of their lives. In some children, the symptoms do not appear until the first or second birthday; others may even go as far as their fifth birthday before they show any symptoms.

Isabella was only eight months old when she was first diagnosed. She had slowly grown fussier, listless, and pale, and she had very little appetite. Apparently, these are the usual symptoms that the medical professionals look for in early diagnosis. Since I was with her daily, I had not noticed these gradual changes.

Children with thalassemia grow and develop slowly, as the body is not getting enough oxygen. Because the treatment is regular blood transfusions, over time major organs, such as the liver, pancreas, spleen, and heart, develop serious problems. The heart has to work harder to pump more red blood cells to the tissues of the body. Overwork enlarges and strains the heart. Heart failure is a serious and sometimes fatal problem; it was in Isabella's case.

Over the years, bone marrow, which is where the body manufactures new blood cells to replace those that are destroyed daily, is also overworked and enlarges in order to cope with the deficiency. The marrow takes more and more bone space so that the bone walls become thin and brittle. This can distort facial bones, which is why, in some ways, children with this disease may look alike.

Bone marrow transplants have been performed with the best results when the donor match is a sibling and the child receiving the transplant is under fifteen years of age. Getting a perfect match is rare, because, in my experience, families that have one child with thalassemia major are usually more cautious about having a large family, owing to the burden that the disease places on each family member.

Red blood cells have a short life span; they live only about four months and must be constantly replaced. Therefore, the fresher the blood is at the time of the transfusion, the better. New blood cells replace the old daily. The old and damaged cells are removed from the blood by the spleen and liver. Because children with this disease have so many damaged cells, the spleen becomes abnormally large, and the liver may not be able to function properly.

Isabella's spleen had become very large during the first few months of her life, and after a great deal of consideration, medical personnel decided to have her spleen removed at the early age of nine months. This was a very serious operation for such a young child. She had to have antibiotics from then on to avoid any possible infections due to the spleen removal.

Children born with thalassemia major survive by being treated with regular blood transfusions—usually monthly. Unfortunately, these regular transfusions, needed for survival, cause other problems.

Iron accumulates in the body when the red blood cells break down. Iron is an essential element for our bodies; however, for thalassemia patients, the excess iron accumulates in the heart, liver, and other organs until they are too damaged and weak to work properly and death occurs. Iron overload can be reduced by a drug called Desferal (deferoxamine mesylate USP), known as the iron chelating agent. It removes iron from the body by helping the kidneys excrete increased amounts of iron, reducing the risk associated with iron overload. An infusion pump, worn daily for eight to ten hours, is one of the most effective and one of the most tolerated treatments for the majority of patients with iron overload. It is a horrendously cumbersome, time-consuming, and expensive treatment.

Researchers have found a new oral drug, Deferasirox (Exjade), to remove the excess iron, but this drug yielded less favorable results than Desferal. It is more costly and is also known to have side effects that are not tolerated by some patients. A third method of chelation, which is used in Europe and the Middle East, is a combination of Desferal and Exjade

Other methods have been used with much less success, such as L-1, which causes severe kidney damage if not properly managed. Therefore, some countries, including Canada, are not allowing its use.

I'm happy to see that treatment has improved considerably and is better managed since Isabella's diagnosis. Although life expectancy has increased significantly over the years, it is rare, even now, for patients to be cured of thalassemia.

Raising a child and knowing that her life would be short has taught Pat and me, as a couple, to constantly live in the moment and be thankful for the good times and hang on to them, because the bad ones are sure to be just around the corner. It taught us to be kind to each other, to forgive each other, to give each other support and understanding, and most of all, to keep on loving each other.

What I am most grateful for is that I don't think this experience has made me bitter or sorry for myself. At least I don't recall having any pity parties. I never questioned, "Why me?" I felt that this was a master plan from higher up that was destined to happen and that one day I would find out why and understand. I also feel blessed for this experience because it has deepened my faith in God. I have learned to accept certain things and make the best of different situations. I often say to myself, "If I have survived the suffering and death of my daughter, I can survive anything." This is my personal belief, and I have been using this philosophy in many other areas of my everyday life.

Pat, Peter, and I have grieved deeply, but we have also loved, and still love, deeply. I am blessed to have had a loving relationship with my husband of over forty years.

We are all given a choice as to how we are going to handle any life situation. We cannot always control the outcome, but we all have the power to choose our actions or reactions. I guess that my husband and I decided to act rather than react, because not only have we survived, but our experience has also made us more empathetic toward others.

## My Roots and My Country

As the eighth of nine children, I did not have much room in my childhood for privacy or individuality. I never gave it much thought, either. That's the way it was.

There is no medical study that I know of in which thalassemia minor's side effects are detected and monitored. So I will never know if my difficulties in school were due to the fact that I carried the disease.

My mother tried so hard to keep me healthy, both physically and mentally, but it couldn't have been easy for her with such a large family. The food variety at the time wasn't so great, in addition to the fact that I was a vegetarian, which made it more challenging for me to have a well-balanced meal.

Despite my poor health and diet, I survived near death from pneumonia, which kept me home in bed for what seemed to be months. I feel that even that experience was part of a divine plan that prepared me for what was to follow later as an adult because in spite of the severity of my condition, I never lost my sense of humor or my spirit of survival.

As my mother often reminded me, what I lacked in physical strength I made up for in mental strength. Even so, the illness put me behind in school, for by the time I was well enough to return, I was too far behind and consequently had to repeat the grade.

My arrival in Canada as an immigrant was a new, exciting, and wonderful beginning, but it was not without its challenges. I walked several blocks to school in the bitter cold Montreal winter, in charge of my younger sister, nephew, and niece. I took charge and held my head up high even when I was yet again placed back two years because my command of English was nil; I had to tough it out. At age twelve, when my family and I emigrated from Italy, I vowed to myself that I would master the English language like a Canadian-born, and I did.

I can still hear the snickering and whispering of my classmates when our names and birthdays are called out loud. I know all about the bullying that we are all aware of in many of today's schools. I looked much younger than twelve, and everyone was surprised when my age was out in the open. I felt so embarrassed I wanted to crawl under my desk and hide.

Eventually, I became proficient in the English language; however, formal education was not my primary goal. As my friends later pointed out, I got my education at the school of hard knocks. Knowing that my formal education was brief made me continually seek and improve my knowledge in all other areas of my life as well; this desire continued during my adult life. I later discovered that success in life is not necessarily determined by education, but rather by effort, goodwill, and attitude.

My father always placed his family's needs before his own. He saw how unprepared we were for that long winter walk to elementary school, especially in our unsuitable winter clothes. To this day, I have kept my red and white scarf and hat (with a pom-pom) to remind me of how far I have come.

Father quickly put a plan into action to build our own house by pooling all of his available resources. This new home was built a stone's throw away from the elementary school— what a treat! We could even go home for lunch if we wanted to.

The new home was great; it accommodated my two married sisters with their families, one in each suite above us. The holidays were filled with close family and cousins. At Christmas time we didn't exchange gifts, but one year one of my brothers surprised each one of us with a beautifully wrapped gift. We all got silly gifts, but the most fun was the unwrapping of them all—the content was irrelevant.

My family was now all together, with the exception of my eldest brother, who was married and settled with a family of his own in Italy. We all missed him terribly, but most of the time we were happy. We did not need much; we had each other, and that was all that mattered.

I did not stay in school long, nor did I graduate from high school. Against my father's wishes, I went to work full-time at different menial jobs in factories or anywhere that I could find work. But the longing for a higher education to better myself never diminished. I enrolled in evening classes. I moved up quickly within the manufacturing company in which I was employed. I had added responsibilities and was satisfied with my job. This made my life much easier, as I was eager to learn, and my environment was pleasant, which made me very happy. I was content and ready to move forward with my life.

Even after a childhood filled with ups and downs that tended to seem like dramatic situations to a young girl, I could now look back and accept that it was just part of life and growing up. Adjusting to a new country, a new language, a new school, and new friends at the awkward age of twelve may have been a little overwhelming. Again, my deep faith in God carried me during the hard times and prepared me for what was yet to come. I knew that He would always look out for me as long as I did the best I could in any given situation. I knew He would bring the right people to me, including the man with whom I would share my life and start a family. And yes, my prayers were answered.

# Chapter Three

## Getting Married and Growing Up Fast

Pasquale swept me off my feet, not only with his charm and good looks, but with his intelligence, wit, and articulate nature.

We shared the same values and backgrounds. We were born in the same village situated in the rolling hills of Calabria, Italy. But our similarities ended there. Our personalities were so very different, and that was what made our relationship work so well. It was a short courtship; from the moment we met, we both knew we had found our life partner. After a brief engagement, we were married, within a year of our first meeting. Marriage for me was something unique and special, and with a young girl's attitude, I told myself that I was not about to make the same mistakes that some of the people I knew had made. I was not judging them but rather learning from the experiences of others around me. I thought my life was almost complete, now that I had started the next phase of my adult life, with a man that was handsome and smart and often spoke in favor of women's rights. Most of all, we had love and respect for each other.

The attributes that we both brought into the marriage were the foundation of a strong relationship that would sustain us in the years to come. We were both ready for a family and parenthood. Less than two years after we married, we became proud parents of a healthy baby boy, whom we named Peter, after his paternal grandfather, as was the custom.

My mother-in-law and father-in-law were ecstatic to become grandparents for the first time. My parents were just as happy for us, but they already had ten grandchildren. What mattered the most to them was that the child was healthy and happy, which was evident in his pleasant disposition.

The only thing that could be better than this was to have a baby girl as well. This wish became a reality two years, less than fourteen days, later.

On October 7, 1971, Isabella was born. So intense was our excitement at this new arrival that we were bursting with happiness. Since Pat had been brought up in a household with four boys—he is the eldest—he was eager to communicate the news of our daughter in a letter to his parents, but in the midst of the excitement, he forgot to stamp it. The letter never made it to its destination.

Another unusual incident was the malfunction of the camera at the time of Isabella's birth, which meant no hospital baby pictures. This was trivial, I thought; our little family felt complete. Looking back on this today, I think that maybe it was a sign that this child's life was not going to be easy.

Two months prior to Peter's birth, Pat's eighteen-year-old brother, Frank, had joined us from Italy. Peter grew up looking up to him more as a big brother than an uncle. Frank was the first addition to our extended family and was soon followed by his fourteen-year-old brother, Luigi when Isabella was two years old.

My household was certainly a busy one, but I was happy. Both Frank and Luigi had big hearts; they were courteous and always willing to give Pat and me a helping hand. Frank was working as a mechanic and made sure that our vehicle was always in good running condition, and he had this tremendous ability to light up a room with his presence. Luigi was a full-time student and worked part-time. Pat was busy working and being an excellent provider.

Frank and Luigi were happy to come to Canada and start a new life, and it was exciting for Pat, because now his two brothers were living under the same roof, and he hoped that eventually his parents would follow. However, that was not in the cards. My father-in-law's health was failing which made it impossible for him to immigrate to Canada.

Of course, as in many families, there was some rivalry between the two children. One time I was doing laundry, and Peter quietly sneaked a bottle of bleach out of the room and poured a generous amount of it over the chocolate-brown sofa. His action made us all realize that Peter was also in great need of attention. I constantly kept this in mind during the following years when Isabella was sick, needing regular blood transfusions and away in the hospital for long periods of time.

My pregnancy with Peter had been healthy, and I had been active up to and including the last day, when Pat and I danced for most of the evening at my cousin's wedding. In the early hours of the next morning I went into labor, giving birth to a 7 lb. 8 oz. baby boy.

But my pregnancy with Isabella was turbulent, to say the least. Iron deficiency was one but one complication. Painful iron injections were administered regularly to boost my hemoglobin (the protein molecule in red blood cells that carries oxygen). At the time all the difficulties with my pregnancy were attributed to a busy household that included a toddler under two years old, my brother-in-law Frank, and my hardworking husband. Although the men were both attentive and helpful in any way they could be, it was still difficult.

Shortly after giving birth, I learned I had gallstones, which explained the excruciatingly painful attacks that started within days of delivering Isabella. Due to my low hemoglobin level, surgery had to wait until I felt stronger.

It was a matter of weeks before I was well enough to undergo the scheduled surgery. Everything proceeded better than expected, but it meant that Isabella could not be breastfed as Peter was. I could not hold her in my arms, which was very disappointing, as she was always crying after we arrived home from the hospital.

But I managed with the help of a housekeeper and my mother, who, although ill herself with a heart condition, was at my side to lend a helping hand. Having given birth to eleven children, she clearly understood my need for help. And my determination to get better always got me through the rough days.

The little one-bedroom apartment where we lived was getting crowded, with three adults and two children, but there was no lack of imagination to make it warm and cozy for all of us. The living room was divided in two by a curtain for privacy, and it became Frank's bedroom. It was small, but it had a window that gave it lots of sunlight. The main bedroom accommodated Isabella in the baby carriage, converted into a bassinet, and Peter in his baby crib. Needless to say, although the room was a large one, it was crowded. The apartment held many happy memories, and there is an abundance of pictures of those happy occasions as proof. But we still needed to move into a larger home and quickly.

So, together with Frank, we pooled our resources and bought an old house. This was the third time that we helped each other financially. The first time was to buy a good-quality camera to take pictures of our growing family, the second time was to buy a car we shared, and the third was to purchase a house we could call home. We totally gutted and remodeled the interior, and it became our little "palace." Pat put all of his talents and expertise to work.

The new house was great. Isabella had her own room, with pink curtains and all the frills of a little girl's room. Peter was now almost three years old and shared a room with his twenty-year-old uncle Frank, and later with his fourteen-year-old uncle Luigi.

Early one morning I was horrified to discover Peter was missing. In a state of panic, I quickly grabbed the sleeping Isabella from her crib and scoured the neighborhood looking for him, but he was nowhere to be found.

I was quickly becoming hysterical when my phone rang. It was my mother telling me that the police had picked Peter up, and when they asked where he was going, he had simply informed them that he was going to work around the corner at the gas station with his uncle Frank. He was equipped with his father's hard hat and his lunch box, containing a peanut butter sandwich. It was obvious to the police what was going on.

When I got the news that he was fine, I was both relieved and angry at the same time. I'm sure many mothers can relate to these mixed feelings. Peter remained with my mother long enough for me to calm down.

My mother was also babysitting another grandson, Lui, the same age as Peter. To this day, Peter and Lui refer to each other not only as cousins but also as "crib buddies."

## *Isabella's Diagnosis*

By now we were settled in our newly renovated home, and I was recuperating nicely from my surgery, so it was time to baptize Isabella. The date was set, and an abundance of food and sweets were prepared to host the entire family and close friends for the coming Sunday.

On the Friday evening before the baptism, Isabella did not look well. We had visited our family doctor just a few days prior, and he had reassured us that she was just fine. As days went by, my mother questioned that Isabella was restless, pale, sleeping more than she should, and had very little appetite.

I will never forget my mother's words: "Serafina, I hear what the doctor told you, but this child does not look well to me; something is wrong." My mother had a point. During the last two months, Isabella had changed; I had seen the gradual change but convinced myself that all was well.

We wanted to make sure that Isabella was going to be well enough for the baptism celebration. By the time we made the decision to take her to the doctor again, it was too late in the day, so the only other choice was to go to the Children's Emergency Hospital.

It was pouring rain; it seemed that Mother Nature was roaring with thunder and lightning. We reached what we thought was the Montreal Children's Emergency Hospital, only to find out later that it was the Jewish General Hospital.

This mistake turned out to be a blessing because there we found, in my opinion, the best doctors in the country and received the best care from all the staff. The first doctor in the emergency room took one look at Isabella and knew at once that she was one sick child; I could read it in his eyes. He told us that she would stay overnight, and he would run some tests. My gut feeling told me that there was something terribly wrong. The mother's instinct kicked into full gear.

The test results showed that her hemoglobin was below five, much below the normal of at least twelve. More tests were needed. More days went by. Finally, all test results were in, and the intern was ready to explain to me what was wrong. What followed next was a mother's worst nightmare; everything seemed to proceed in slow motion. The severity of her condition did not hit me until he was finished giving me all the facts.

The young doctor with flaming red hair had the enormous task of breaking the news to me. I was on my own at the hospital. Pat had gone to work and left me with Isabella. Arrangements were made for Peter to stay with my mother. This young intern took me into his office and explained her condition calmly and professionally.

It was too much information for me to wrap my head around. All I could remember was that she would need regular blood transfusions. At first, I said, "Well, that doesn't sound so bad; we can adjust to that." He then went on to explain that the side effects were serious and could result in death at an early age.

It was 1971 and the available statistics showed that children affected with this illness, called beta thalassemia major, had a short life span and most likely would die in their teen years. Few children made it to adulthood.

Everything was a blur after that. It felt like I was in a fog-filled tunnel. I only had one request of this young man— that he break the news to Pat when he came in because I just did not know how I was going to explain to him what I had just been told.

I thought that the best person to call was Isabella's godmother, my very good, long-time friend, Mariantonia. All of my other family members were busy with their own lives and families, and I did not want to tell them until I could process all this information on my own.

I explained to Mariantonia in between sobs what was happening, and before I knew it, she was there by my side, lending all of the support I could ask from a friend. To this day, Mary and I share a special bond unlike that with any other friend. Mary was there by my side at the best of times and the worst of times in my life.

# Chapter Five

*The Hospital; Our Second Home*

Isabella's hospital stay turned from days to weeks, and then she was in and out for months. By the time she was stable enough to have the reception for her baptism, the church ceremony was only a formality, and the party that followed was only to have some fun and celebrate life.

We were all so grateful to God for keeping her alive, because she had been close to death twice, and we would learn to take her medical condition one day at a time. We all needed to take baby steps to accept her condition and to always keep a positive attitude. Over the years that followed, this became our family way of life.

Isabella almost slipped away from us the first time she was taken to the hospital on that stormy Friday night. She was already in critical condition. After receiving many units of blood, there were other complications. We did not know if she would make it through the night. Being Catholic, we called our priest to administer the last rites and to baptize her at the same time. But she bounced back; she was not ready to give up yet.

It was such a heart-wrenching experience to see my little girl, so small and helpless, being probed over and over again to find healthy veins for continuous transfusions. By the time she was out of the hospital, she had five incisions—one on each arm, one on one ankle, and two on the other—and a large scar on her scalp.

One time I walked into Isabella's room and found her two little hands bound to the crib so that she would not remove the needle from her scalp. With a heavy heart, I took her in my arms and gently rocked her to sleep.

The only time the nurses would free her hands was when I held her in my arms and kept her hands from pulling out the needle. I eventually had to put her back in her bed and go home, but her hands had to be bound again.

On returning to the hospital the next day, I found her with a red-and-blue patch on her scalp where the needle had been inserted; apparently, something had gone wrong during the night. There was a laceration on her scalp of about two inches in diameter where her hair had been shaved in order to transfuse into one of her larger veins.

This experience turned out to be one of the many traumatic times because it left Isabella with a scar on the scalp where the hair follicles were too damaged for the hair to ever grow back.

All through her short life, this scar was a reminder of those times in the hospital. Now, on the scale of importance, a small bald spot was definitely not at the top of the list of worries, but it always made Isabella self-conscious, and she developed this habit of automatically covering the area with her hand and pulling her hair over it. Particularly as Isabella got older, this became more important to her.

I am grateful to a very talented hairstylist by the name of Helen, who knew exactly what to do to solve the problem of Isabella's bald spot. We followed her all over the city to be able to get an appointment with her.

During the last weeks of intensive and continuous transfusions that saved her life, Isabella's spleen had become so enlarged that after careful consultations by the medical staff, they decided that it was best to have it removed. On the day that the staff was to make this decision, a meeting was held that included all of the interns and nurses, as this was a teaching hospital. The auditorium was packed, and there was Isabella, at center stage with a bow attached to a few strands of hair on top of her head. She was the subject of a discussion—the pros and cons of the splenectomy.

This was not a decision that was taken lightly, although it is common for thalassemia patients to have the spleen removed. The concern was that Isabella's condition had been barely stabilized, and at such a young age (only nine months old) the procedure was very risky. After much consideration and weighing all of the pros and cons, surgery was scheduled to take place as soon as possible.

We waited anxiously through the long hours for the outcome of the procedure. The angels must have been cheering for her again because she recuperated quickly and continued to thrive and grow like any normal, healthy child. At one point after the surgery, she gained so much weight that you would never have known that it was the same child who only months ago was so thin.

When the baptism took place, we had many reasons to celebrate. Isabella's condition was now stabilized, and the scheduled monthly transfusions had become a way of life. Her little body was like a road map, marked with the journey of her enormous challenge.

One day, after coming home from one of her scheduled transfusions, she had so much energy that while playing in our backyard on the swing set that Pat had made especially for the children, she fell flat on her face, landing on a pebble that injured her forehead right between her eyes. At times we joked about the scar and called it her "third eye."

Back to the emergency department again, where we were met by the same intern who had looked after her just hours earlier. Imagine his surprise when he saw us there and said, "Can't get enough of us? Or did you just miss us and have to come back?" Five stitches later we were off home again, and while the doctor waved goodbye to us, he jokingly said, "Go home and don't come back for a while."

We had now fallen into a routine, and I too was gaining some weight back after dropping to a mere eighty-six pounds during Isabella's long hospital stay. The enormous burden of Isabella's illness and caring for the family had taken its toll on me.

I cannot stress strongly enough the importance of always taking care of your health when you are dealing with serious issues, as it is easy to put yourself last on the list. I am guilty of this. Many times the willpower alone was just not strong enough, but I'm getting better. I have learned to take better care of myself, by carefully monitoring my diet and exercise. However, my emotional state is not always at its best; l still constantly need to remind myself to keep things in perspective, just as I did for years when faced with the everyday challenges with Isabella. One way I achieved perspective was by writing about how Isabella has changed my life.

Every five weeks I would take Isabella for a blood test, which was cross-matched, and then usually by the third day, the hospital would call us to bring her in for the blood transfusion. After the blood was drawn for the cross-match, we always visited the nurses in their lunch room, because they had become like extended family members. During one visit, I said to them that we were in a hurry that morning, as we had left the house in such a rush, and I was anxious to clean up the mess I had left behind. The head nurse made a very good point and said, "Don't give a second thought about the mess, forget the surroundings and how it looks, just enjoy each other's company; play with your children, everything else can wait."

That was a very valuable lesson for me to learn; a practice that I put to use throughout the years to come. Any time I felt overwhelmed by my responsibilities as a mother, I went back to this piece of advice.

We resumed the life of a "normal" family following Isabella's initial diagnosis and her recovery after the spleen surgery. In addition to the regular transfusions, she was given folic acid and antibiotics to prevent infections. For this reason, we were strongly advised to avoid any house pets other than perhaps a goldfish; hence, we opted to have an aquarium with very colorful fish in it. It wasn't until Isabella was seven years old and Peter almost nine that I decided it was time to have pets. Since Peter and Isabella had birthdays two weeks apart, they were each presented with a full-grown cat.

Three and a half years had gone by since Isabella's diagnosis, and the bitter Montreal winters were hard to take. I nervously drove the family car on dangerous icy roads, but only when it was absolutely necessary like the trips to the hospital.

For Pat, being in the construction business and working outdoors was no picnic either. So one day in the spring of 1975, Pat and brother Frank, who was still living in the same household, decided to go to the West Coast and check out what it was like in British Columbia.

This new idea took root one cold winter afternoon while Pat was reading, as he often does in his leisure time. The particular book he was reading gave full details of the geography and weather of Vancouver, stating that it was the warmest spot in Canada, and describing Victoria, with its early spring and colorful cherry blossoms. It seemed too good to be true. It sounded so much like the temperate climate we had left behind in our native home in southern Italy. Smiling widely and pointing to the map of Vancouver, Pat enthusiastically announced, "This is where we are going to live."

## Vancouver, Here We Come

We quickly made airfare arrangements were quickly made, and off went Pat and Frank, to explore the West. It took only a few days for them to be convinced that it was like paradise on earth.

A few days later I received a phone call from a very excited Pat, telling me to start making arrangements to move, because Vancouver was so beautiful he had no doubt that I would love it as much as he did. I began the task of making all the necessary moving arrangements by calling transport companies for quotes, and then the packing began.

My heart was heavy, though; as much as I wanted to move to a new city, I was leaving my siblings, all seven of them, and their families. It was especially difficult to leave my parents, who had done their best to keep the entire family close by, with the exception of my eldest brother, Giovanni, who at an early age had moved from his birthplace of Calabria to the beautiful hills of Tuscany, where he still lives today with his own family.

The three months that preceded our departure from Montreal to British Columbia were filled with chaotic days, even though we were moving within the same country. Nonetheless, we were going from one end of the continent to the other. It may just as well have been another country, it seemed so far away.

All of our furniture and personal belongings were packed in wooden shipping crates as required by the rail company. Pat and I, along with our children—Peter, aged five, and Isabella, aged three— were to travel by car and explore our vast nation of Canada at the same time. Once again, our friend Mariantonia and her husband, Joe, came to our rescue and tried to make our long journey safer by providing us with maps and points of interest, including gas stations and accommodations along the way. The Trans-Canada in 1975 was not what it is today, and with two young children in the car, it was extremely important that we knew exactly where to stop and where the best overnight accommodations were. Frank made sure that our vehicle was in excellent driving condition with the same love and attention as usual.

At the end of each day we would stop, have dinner, and rest, and then start all over again the next day. Our trip across Canada made us appreciate the vast and diverse country that we live in, from the endless kilometers of flat prairies to the rugged mountains of the West Coast.

We finally reached Vancouver on a beautiful Sunday afternoon in June and stopped in an area that we had no idea was called "Little Italy." West Vancouver had a zero vacancy rate, so we were ecstatic when we found a house for rent.

We also had wonderful landlords, Uncle Bruno and Aunt Dorothy, who became close family friends. We have fond memories of them that will remain imprinted in our minds forever. Peter was in charge of walking the landlord's dog, a placid German shepherd, and Isabella was often busy picking berries on the vast property.

Within days of our arrival, all of our furniture arrived in good condition, except for some minor broken items; but what was missing from all of our belongings was Pat's toolbox. As Pat was a carpenter by trade, these tools were essential to his work. Well, all it took was one stern phone call by Uncle Bruno, a lawyer by profession, stating to the person on the other end of the line that if this toolbox did not appear in the next twenty-four hours, there would be serious consequences. The toolbox miraculously appeared the next day.

Pat soon found work, and we would often visit him during the day. In the evening we would take a picnic basket to the park by the beach. The breathtakingly beautiful city softened the ache in our hearts from missing our family so far away.

By the end of the summer we were forced to move again, as the large rental property was being subdivided for condos. As much as we would have liked to stay in the same neighborhood, it was beyond our price range. We decided to settle in the Richmond area, a safe and growing community that was ideal for a young family.

The decision to buy a home was made quickly. We arrived early for the showing of one particular house that was vacant, and we could take a peek through the windows. It was unanimous this was going to be our new home. We proceeded to have a picnic lunch in the half-acre backyard while waiting for the Realtor.

When he arrived and saw our young family having a picnic, it was like a picture postcard, he later told us. He proceeded to do everything in his power to have our offer accepted. And so the next stage of our family life began.

Peter was to start grade one in September, and Isabella was to follow in two years. Seeing her in school was a big step for me toward letting go.

I felt as though the universe was sending me a message when I was faced with the possibility of a third pregnancy, only to discover that the chance of carrying to full term was very slim because the pregnancy had taken place in my fallopian tube. Sure enough, the vision of having a third child quickly became only a fantasy; there could be no other child, ever.

The slow and silent grieving process took a long time for me to overcome because the loss of the pregnancy was never out in the open and therefore not discussed with anyone. I did everything in my power to keep busy with school activities and babysitting. Peter's teacher was looking for someone to care for her newborn so that she could return to her teaching. Her son was only a few months old. We worked out a schedule where she would bring her baby to me and in turn would drive Peter and Isabella to school with her. This was a good arrangement for everyone, at least for a while.

Despite the situation we were in, I still wanted to lend a helping hand to those less fortunate; so, as a family, we decided to become foster parents. The paperwork was completed with the help of our family doctor, and in no time we were approved. It was a matter of a few short weeks when I received a phone call that there was a two-year-old in need of a home.

But once again reality began to set in. How was I to properly care for a two-year-old under these circumstances and, adding to the question, without any family members to help me? Pat and I soon realized that being foster parents was not for us. Besides, my other concern was that I would have difficulty letting go of these children once permanent homes were found.

The years went by quickly, with not much happening other than the usual trips to the hospital for Isabella's transfusions, scheduled so that we would be home before Peter came out of class. At the odd time, Isabella and I would be detained at the hospital much later than anticipated. On these rare occasions, we would come home to find Peter sitting on the front porch waiting for us to come home. It was heart-wrenching because there were very few people I could call on for help in such emergencies.

I had no idea how difficult it was going to be when I left Montreal and ventured out to the West Coast—no family members to count on or close friends. I would often sit on my front porch and cry tears of desperation and loneliness. But, slowly, things began to change.

Eventually, many other family members joined us. The anticipation of their arrival was very exciting. Once they arrived there were major adjustments to be made, because we all lived under the same roof in a very small house until they could find a place of their own. It did not matter; it was great to have family close by again.

For years after, there were additions from both sides of the family. It was wonderful to have them join us on numerous happy occasions and holidays.

*This drawing shows how the pump with the Desferal is placed on the body (usually on the abdomen). The needle on the pump is inserted under the skin, which allows the drug to be distributed through the body. Drawing by Andrea* Autelitano

# *Chapter Seven*

## *The Question*

For the first four to five years in school, Isabella had no problems keeping up with the rest of the class, even though many days of school were missed due to hospital visits. Nevertheless, her medical condition could never be ignored, not even for a moment.

She knew from an early age that she was different. One day, when she was only four years old, she asked me the dreaded question that I knew she would eventually ask— "Mom, when am I going to die?" I was shocked and quickly thought of a simple answer: "Well, sweetie, we are all going to die one day." I understood the question that she was asking me, but she was frustrated by my answer and repeated the question. "No, Mom! When am I going to die?"

At first, I tried to dodge the question, but I realized that she deserved an explanation, one that was appropriate for her age, or else this question would come up again. I had to tell her that I truly did not know when she would die but that due to her medical condition, her life might be short. I emphasized that all four of us were going to live our lives to the fullest as if each day was our very last.

She needed no more explanations after this, and she never asked that question again. Even though Isabella seemed to be satisfied with my answer, it felt as if a knife had cut through my heart. To help us get through the tough times, we reasoned that life has no guarantees and that any one of us could experience a fatal accident and life would be over.

Isabella understood this because Pat and I had already adopted this philosophy (more so since her diagnosis). We were going to do the best we could to enjoy her as long as we were destined to have her.

The reality was that we all pretended not to see the elephant in the room. But one thing was for sure—none of us would give up hope that a cure, or at least a better treatment regime and understanding of Isabella's condition, would one day be possible. For now, we would take one day at a time live our life to the fullest, and have fun!

Isabella knew she had different challenges than her friends. But how do you explain to a four-year-old that her life will be short and that it is likely going to end in her teen years? We believed this because, at the time, this was the prognosis given to most thalassemia patients.

There was very little reading material available that explained side effects and other challenges that we would be dealing with. I was always on the lookout for possible articles or books on the subject other than the verbal explanations given to us by the medical staff.

During one of Isabella's scheduled transfusions, I was excited to find an article in Readers' Digest as I was thumbing through the magazines in the waiting room. The story was written by a mother of two children, both with thalassemia major. The article stated that one of the children had quietly passed away during the night while sleeping.

This story touched me beyond words. Once again, I was grateful that at least one of my children was not affected by thalassemia and was perfectly healthy. This story was also a source of consolation for me because it did not have any details about the child being in distress but only that the child died peacefully while sleeping.

From that day forward, until Isabella died, I made it a point every single night, before I went to bed, to peek in her bedroom and listen to her to see if she was asleep and breathing. On occasion, I could hear her snore, and with a smile on my face, I'd thank God she was alive for one more day.

Thanks to modern science and research in recent years, the prognosis for thalassemia has changed. Many patients are now living well into their thirties and forties and can live happy, normal, and productive lives. With careful medical care, many can also have children.

Patients affected by this illness have the tremendous challenge of balancing their studies or careers and maintaining their mental and physical health at its optimum. Lack of knowledge about thalassemia still exists; that is why a support system is crucial for both family members and the medical profession.

Our challenge as parents was to find a balance between treating Isabella as a normal healthy child with a future to look forward to and making each day count while being on the alert for any health changes or complications. She was a popular child who excelled in school and in her other activities, such as ballet, gymnastics, tap dancing, and learning to play the piano.

Isabella was treated equally by her peers and teachers. Toward the end of her fourth and fifth week after a blood transfusion, there were signs of her struggling to keep up with her schedule, and that was a sensitive issue because sometimes she needed to say no to some activities and pay extra attention to her health. She would need to rest more and make sure she ate a well-balanced diet. In some ways, we all benefit by being aware of our health developing good eating habits and always taking good care of ourselves.

This was one of the few things that we had control over. Therefore, we all made sure that we followed the same schedule.

Strict regiments of blood transfusions continued every four to five weeks for Isabella until the age of ten. The blood transfusions would probably have been every two to three weeks if her spleen had not been removed.

I could not have asked for a better team of committed medical professionals to take care of Isabella. Competent and caring hematologists, a team of loving, gentle nurses, and a supportive secretary at the clinic where Isabella spent so much of her time made it feel like her second home.

Maintaining a sense of humor always helped in any situation. We would make light of it when it was time for another blood transfusion by saying, "Time to go fill up again," just like when filling up a tank at the gas station.

Isabella's blood transfusions left marks on her hands that were clearly visible. Her small body told a harsh story. Her left hand had the largest vein, which was used regularly for transfusions. Although it was scarred and her skin bruised, it worked well every single time, without fail. The usual nurses knew better than to question Isabella about using this particular vein.

Whenever a new nurse would say, "We will give this vein a rest and use another one this time," Isabella would softly reply, "No, this one on my left-hand works very well." But they would try a new one anyway and, after a few failed attempts, would inevitably go back to the usual vein. Isabella would comment under her breath, "I told you this one was the best one!"

The same story would repeat itself every time unless I intervened or the nurses from the clinic staunchly confirmed what Isabella was saying.

It is rare to find a person who has not had a blood test at some point, and we know that most of us don't like needles. But that is a small poke, and it's over before we know it. On Isabella, they used a needle large enough for an entire transfusion of two units of blood at a time, and it took many hours.

So, at the end of the day, when it was all over and there was no negative reaction to the blood transfusion, Isabella was full of endless energy. It was as though she was given a new lease on life—

at least for a few more weeks anyway. We were filled with gratitude and thought, "Another successful transfusion!" Everything else was trivial.

But there were signs that Isabella's health was changing. Her body had developed so many antibodies that it became more and more difficult to find a perfect blood match. This meant a longer waiting period from the cross-match to the actual blood transfusion; consequently, Isabella felt tired to the point of not being able to fully function at times.

Her skin pigmentation was affected by the numerous blood transfusions, and her skin tone changed to a dark grey. This change occurs because the body uses up all the healthy blood cells, and iron accumulates in the system. The excess iron gets deposited in the major organs such as the liver, pancreas, and heart, which over time causes these organs to shut down.

It was time to make some changes to her treatment regimen. We knew that Europe had been using an iron-chelating drug called Desferal, which helped to remove the excess iron from the body. But we also knew that it was very intrusive. This drug would need to be used on a daily basis seven days a week (for eight to ten hours a day), taking a break only one evening a week. The powder medication would be mixed with distilled water and inserted under the skin. A syringe with tubing was attached to a battery-operated pump that slowly administered the medicine during the night. The particular spot did not matter, as long as the needle was under the skin.

This invasive and, at times, painful procedure became a way of life for Isabella and is still used today for many patients. However, this presented us with a tremendous financial burden, because British Columbia was not one of the provinces willing to accept this new treatment and its high cost.

Hence, our battle commenced, to see to it that those few children in B.C. got this treatment, which would help prolong their lives.

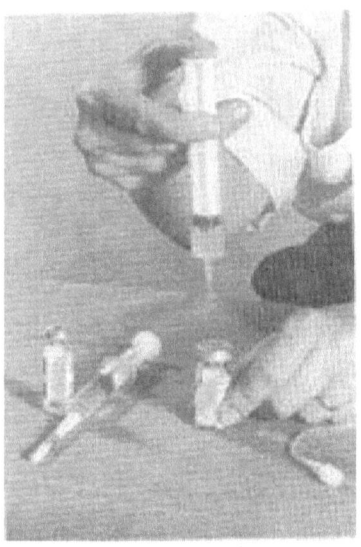

*(top): The first figure shows the addition of distilled water into the Desferal bottle to dissolve the powder, which was then sucked back into the syringe*

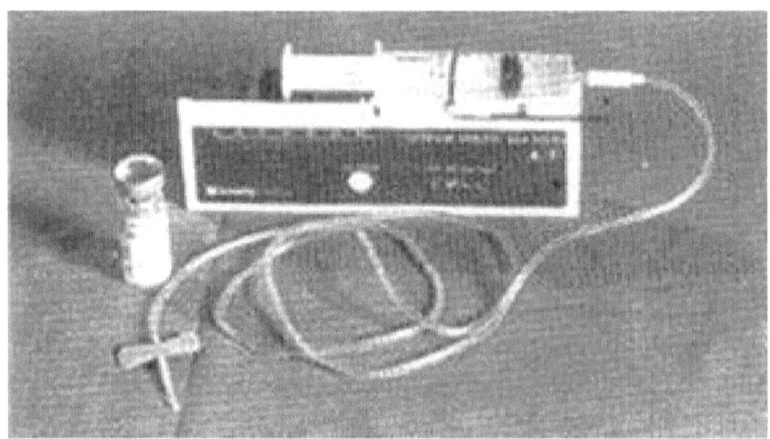

*(bottom): The syringe is attached to the pump, and a long infusion set with a small, sharp needle is inserted underneath the skin to pump the Desferal into the body for a period of about eight hours. Photos from What Is Thalassemia? by Rino Vullo and Bernadette Model*

# Chapter Eight

## Tea Time and Desferal – Our Rituals

We learned that tea had some degree of success in extracting excess iron from the body; so while we were waiting to see results from our government, we encouraged Isabella to drink two to three cups of tea per day. That became our special time together. We would use this method while we were waiting for government approval to pass a law so that Desferal could, and would, be administered by the health care system.

I even bought a special teapot for two for this ritual. To this day, over twenty-five years later, I still have this teapot, and I use it regularly. Only now, I have the tea alone, or, rather, without Isabella's physical presence.

After much lobbying with the help of Isabella's hematologist at the children's hospital, it became law that Desferal could be used in British Columbia. One of the reasons we were given for the reluctance to use Desferal was that it was still experimental, and there was not enough evidence about the side effects and the benefits. But my gut instinct was telling me that there was more to it. I wondered if the government was questioning the expensive treatment because the fate of these children was already known. It seemed to me that patients with thalassemia were receiving the minimum amount of care, almost bordering on neglect, compared to other patients with other illnesses who showed better results from funds and time that was spent on treatment. Isabella's Journey

When approval was finally received, we did not waste any time. Isabella was admitted to the children's hospital to undergo certain tests for assessment and for training so that she and other family members were capable of supervising this new procedure at home.

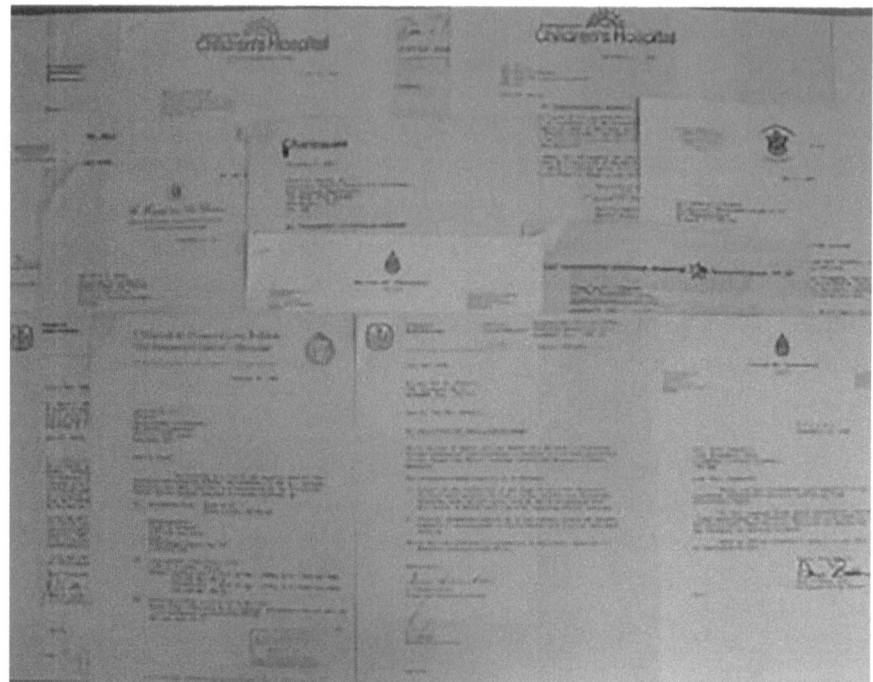

*Numerous letters were sent to various levels of government, urging officials to lobby for coverage for the expensive iron chelating drug Desferal.*

Out came the oranges to practice injections on, and eventually Isabella was sent home with the complete kit to get started. Pat was the first to administer it, and Isabella and I became the assistants to prepare and mix the medication as instructed by the hospital staff. Pat was the one with the steady hand and the precision to insert the needle under the skin. It seemed that the abdominal area was the best for Isabella, although many other children and young adults preferred the arm or the leg.

Shortly after we began using the pump at home, my father came to visit, and as Isabella was preparing for the pump, I noticed my dad slowly walking away. It was too painful for him to watch.

It wasn't long before Isabella took over the responsibility of inserting the needle by herself. She had learned to mix the medication as well.

It took a little coaxing every night and perhaps a reward afterward, like a sip of my coffee, to give her a little encouragement.

We would start every night after dinner at about eight o'clock so that she would have her eight hours of treatment before she had to get ready for school the next morning.

Getting ready for school was another hurdle at the best of times. Hitting the critical pre-teen years is challenging enough for most young girls, but delays in the morning due to the removal of the pump and paying extra attention to her hair so that the bald spot on the side of her head would not be revealed meant that morning preparations took longer than average.

Breakfast, along with her cup of tea, would be ready and waiting for her. As she was usually late for class, we had this procedure where I would swoosh the tea from one cup to another so that it would be just the right temperature for her to quickly gulp down and then run to school.

The notes continued to come from the school, reminding me to get her to school on time. I can now understand their point of view about why it was important, but at the time I was disappointed at how rigid they were even though I had explained to all of her teachers about Isabella's health issues.

I really blew a fuse one day when Isabella came home with a note from one of her teachers (who later became the vice principal) saying that if she continued to be late for school, it would go on her school records, and that would not look good when she went out into the workforce.

I immediately requested a meeting with the teacher, but she remained unmoved by the circumstances and said that rules were rules, that they were to be obeyed, and that no exceptions would be made for Isabella. I told her that Isabella's tardiness was the least of my concerns and was terribly disappointed that this woman, whom I considered an excellent teacher, lacked human understanding and warmth.

I lost all respect for her after that. Isabella died less than a year after this incident, and everyone at the school was shocked, including this particular teacher.

These were the quiet little battles that we had to endure and deal with on a daily basis. It was hard for others to understand that even though Isabella looked well, had a good attitude, and was very sensitive to other people's needs, she was, in fact, very ill, and her health could take a turn for the worse at any time.

I am told by patients and their families that the lack of knowledge and understanding of thalassemia still exists today in the education system.

Today other forms of chelation therapy have been developed; Exjade, L1, and Deferiprone can be taken orally, but it seems that Desferal is still the chelation of choice by most doctors.

Deferiprone has been recently approved by US FDA for iron chelation, just as in the European Union, but it is not yet approved by Health Canada.

This new drug has caused much controversy in Canada. L-1 is an iron-chelating drug that is used in some countries, but it is also known to have side effects such as kidney damage. Exjade, which has minor side effects, is a tablet that can be dissolved in water but is not as effective as Desferal.

This is the first choice by many patients, simply for the freedom it gives. However, this is still not the answer for everyone, because some patients cannot tolerate it. In some cases, Exjade in conjunction with Desferal has produced the best results.

I hear that some patients don't tolerate these new drugs as well as Desferal. And doctors may not prefer the new drugs, because they don't know all of the side effects, or simply because they may be more costly than Desferal.

All of the above reasons may be true and perfectly legitimate, but one thing I know for sure is that with the use of Desferal on a daily basis, everyday life becomes more complicated because of its method of application. Yes, it is effective in treating the problem of iron overload, but it comes at a very high personal cost to the individual. More research is needed to develop a method of iron chelation therapy less invasive than what is now available.

Bone marrow transplant is currently the only cure and has become increasingly successful. As I said earlier in the book— and it is worth repeating—for best results, the criteria are that the qualifying child is strong enough to go through the gruesome preparation before the transplant and is preferably under fifteen years old and with a donor sibling.

# *Photographs*

*Serafina and Isabella soaking in the sunshine in
White Rock BC. (1975)*

**Top Left:** Isabella, Peter & Pasquale enjoy a day at the park (1980).
**Top Middle:** Isabella & her charismatic smile (1975).
**Top Right:** Our last family photo (1985).
**Middle Left:** Isabella trying to keep up with her teen peers.
**Middle Right:** Managing a smile for Mickey Mouse during last days in hospital.
**Bottom Left:** Isabella at 2 years old.
**Middle:** Isabella practicing gymnastics.
**Bottom Right:** Isabella's dance recital as "Miss Cutie Pie".
**Bottom:** Isabella (1971).

**Top Left:** Isabella & Peter helping Dad paint.
**Right:** Isabella doing most of the chatting with Peter.
**Middle:** Isabella resting after returning from hospital.
**Bottom Left:** Isabella's 14th birthday.
**Bottom:** Peter & Isabella.
**Bottom Right:** Peter at 2 years holding Isabella.

**Top Left:** Isabella, Peter, Serafina & Uncle Giovanni Campolongo, in Tuscany.
**Right:** Grandfather, Peter Sammarco, with Peter and Isabella, in Italy.
**Second Row:** Isabella's baptism with godparents, Mariantonia & Joe Moreno; a celebration including grandmother, Maria Luisa Campolongo (second from right middle picture).

**Right:** Pasquale, Serafina & Peter enjoy family time in Victoria, BC (2008).
**Below:** Isabella, Uncle Luigi, Serafina, Uncle Frank, Pasquale & Peter (1974).
**Bottom:** Isabella welcomed home from the hospital by Peter & Dad (1971).
**Bottom Right:** Serafina & Isabella soaking in the sunshine (1975).

# *Chapter Nine*

*Lending a Helping Hand*

In order that we stay balanced as a couple, Pat and I would often take the time to go out for dinner, and dance when time allowed—just the two of us on a regular basis. But when the time in between outings was too long, our children would take matters into their own hands and make babysitting arrangements.

Both Peter and Isabella knew how challenging it was for us as parents, so much so that they could see before we did when it was time for Pat and me to take some time off to replenish our energy. They would say, "It is time for the two of you to go out again. We took care of everything; you are going out this evening."

This was our way of coping because it is so easy to get lost in the everyday responsibilities of a family, let alone one with special needs. We had seen too many couples break up under such strain. Maintaining that sense of balance between daily responsibilities and hope for a better future was tricky. We never wanted to feel like victims of our circumstances.

In my family, we learned early on that although money is an essential commodity, it most definitely is not the most important aspect of life and need not take precedence over family, friends, and community. With this concept in mind, we raised Isabella without spoiling her, and she became our teacher in learning how to live and, most importantly, to help others during their life's journeys.

When Isabella was about eleven years old, we were having our usual family meeting that took place every Sunday evening, where each family member shared what was on their minds. The main subject was deciding whether to allow Isabella's sixteen-year-old cousin to come and live with us for a while. Pat and I were a little reluctant to take on this added responsibility.

Without any hesitation and with such conviction, Isabella said, "What is there to think about? She needs help and she asked for our help. She wants to come and stay with us for a while—end of story."

She made it sound so simple. When someone needs help, you reach out and help. Her cousin did come and live with us for a few months until she was ready to move back with her own parents.

Isabella's short, condensed life helped all who met her—especially Pat, Peter, and me—appreciate being alive and enjoy even the smallest things of beauty. We experienced the deepest sorrow and the highest happiness in life. In my opinion, unless one goes through some deeply emotional experiences, one cannot truly appreciate how beautiful life can be.

I also learned, a very long time ago, to keep things in perspective, to differentiate what is really important and what is not so important, and not to put so much emphasis on trivial matters.

Now, years later, when I'm not dealing with life-and-death situations as I did when Isabella was alive, I catch myself. Sometimes during our normal, everyday ups and downs, I try not to dramatize or I will talk to myself and say, "That's not so bad; I can get through this challenge." Because I have handled my daughter's sufferings and got past that, I can certainly manage whatever the difficulty may be at any given time.

It is easy to get caught up in everyday drama, whether it is our own or that of other people. I find that the more we over-dramatize and feed into small problems, the bigger they become.

One day another mother and I were picking up our children from elementary school, and I couldn't help but notice how agitated and upset she was; so I asked what was wrong. She told me she was so worried because that morning her child had the symptoms of the beginning of a cold, and she was anxious to see if her child had gotten better or worse during the day. She went on and on about how terrible her daughter felt when she had a cold.

I had to stop myself from making a comment about what I was really thinking of this drama queen. Here I was, waiting for Isabella to come out of class to drive her to the hospital to get cross-matched for her next blood transfusion.

But at the same time, I also understood and sympathized with this mother for feeling so helpless and worried. I could not compare her situation to mine. This young mother was just as concerned over her child as I was over Isabella. I had to remember that maybe she had never experienced anything more serious than a child with a cold. This was just one of the many scenarios that I encountered over the years. I developed a tough skin and learned to keep things in perspective for Isabella's survival.

# Chapter Ten

*Growth Hormone Therapy*

An area of concern for many children affected by thalassemia major is their slow growth. Isabella's friends were growing into their teen years, but she was about twelve inches shorter than all of them. She became more and more self-conscious of her height and growth development. We began to question her doctors and explore available options.

They advised us to wait a little longer and monitor her growth more closely because her small stature could also have been inherited from Pat and me. This explanation may have been a valid one, but I also felt that it may have been just an excuse to postpone the costly tests. I tried my best to rationalize that this made sense; so we waited about six months. In the meantime, a series of tests was scheduled for the Christmas holidays when she was out of school, to avoid more absent school days.

The tests took just over a week to complete. The results were in, but it was again decided it was too early to administer any growth hormones because there was still a chance she would grow without any outside medical interference. This meant that all of those tests, which were not that pleasant, would probably be repeated at a later date.

The excruciating joint pains that continued throughout Isabella's short life and often woke her up in the middle of the night were attributed to the side effects of thalassemia. To make light of it, we used to call them growing pains, because she looked so well soon after she was stabilized with her treatments.

More months went by, and she tried very hard to keep up with her friends and their activities, such as exploring taking public transit on their own. After a couple of times, she admitted to me that she would not join her friends again on the bus, because it was too hard, although she remained in good spirits most of the time, even cheering her friends up when they were down.

She quietly kept this information from her friends about not being able to go on public transportation.

I was later told by her classmates that lunchtime was a blast with Issy, as she was called by her friends. Her laughter could be heard all the way down the hall to the other end of the school.

She was always ready and willing to lend a helping hand to others in need, such as the time she was in elementary school and the principal requested my permission to ask for Isabella's help in trying to reach out to a new student in the school that was having a difficult time. He said that if anyone could do it, Isabella could, since she was so friendly and caring. He was right. This school principal was one of the very few intuitive people in the school system who really knew and cared for his students. He got to know each of them personally, rather than just as a number.

Isabella and Debbie soon became best friends. This worked out very well, because Debbie was almost twice the size of Isabella, and Debbie began to look out for her when she was not feeling well. She gave Issy her physical and moral support. Unfortunately, this friendship ended the next year when Debbie moved to a nearby island. Although they kept in touch, they were too far apart to spend more time together.

This goes to show us all that if we can reach out and help others, it comes back to us tenfold. There were great times for Isabella in elementary school, unlike high school, where the curriculum and peer pressure made it difficult without her best friend close.

Isabella needed to adjust and make new friends there. Peter was in the same school. He became very protective of his sister and even got into a fight or two over her. Peter was encouraged to solve any issues at school without fighting, but when the issue dealt with his sister, his brotherly love and protectiveness came out in full force. They were very close siblings. At age six and four, Peter and Isabella proudly announced that when they grew up, they would find an apartment of their own and live together.

Peter was very popular in school and very involved in sports. When Isabella began to make more friends, she quickly caught on that some girls were only hanging around her to be close to Peter. She was also very quick to set the record straight as to who were her true friends.

Parties of enormous numbers of students were held at the family home, well organized by both of them, along with the help of a few chosen friends. These friends would sit and talk with Isabella for extensive amounts of time and enjoy her company.

# Chapter Eleven

*Japan and Hawaii*

Peter had a keen interest in Japan after participating in a student exchange program through the school. He and Isabella made very good friends with one exchange student in particular, and Peter still keeps in touch with her to this day. She is one of the top surgeons in Japan.

Consequently, when it was time for the next group of students to be chosen for the Japan exchange, Isabella was willing and ready to embrace the same experience that her brother had a year earlier. But this was not to be, because the school felt Isabella was a high-risk candidate, and they were not willing to accept her as one of the students for the exchange program. It felt as though now it was convenient for the school to point out the seriousness of her illness, but not when she was late for school.

Isabella was crushed by the news. She was sad and disappointed. I was furious, but there was nothing I could do to change their minds. The decision was made. Of course now, years later, I can understand the school's concern.

The school had every right to decline including her in the program, but at the time I felt that the school had two sets of rules, both of which would accommodate the school and teachers but not take into account the individual student or the family.

That year Pat decided that it was time to take a family Christmas vacation to Hawaii, even though we could not really afford it; the overall morale of the entire family was that important. With all the excitement and preparations for the trip to Hawaii, the disappointment of the Japanese student exchange was soon forgotten.

We had a great time in Hawaii. Isabella would step out onto the balcony of our hotel, take a deep breath, admire the view, and say, "Now, this is the life!" This has become another family motto.

The family vacations were always highly charged with mixed emotions, happy and sad. Again we tried to savor every moment together. Peter and Isabella would venture out on their own, shopping and strengthening the bond they had and at times having their arguments. Isabella would always win these verbal battles. Pat and I would watch them and think to ourselves, "Will this be our last vacation together?"

That Christmas was indeed the last vacation for the four of us, but the wonderful memories will last forever.

As soon as we returned home, we quickly got back to our daily routine. Time went so fast that before we knew it, it was spring again, with all its glorious blossoms and all the activities that go with it, especially at school.

Isabella tried very hard in school, but she had numerous days absent and at times had very low energy. We had provided her with a math tutor that helped her keep up with the school curriculum. On one of her scheduled days, her tutor called me to go and pick up Isabella, because she was not up to the lesson and was not well enough to walk home. As she got in the car I asked her how she was feeling, and she calmly replied, "I wasn't feeling very well this afternoon during gym class. I think there is something wrong with my heart, Mom."

"Well," I replied, trying very hard not to show my panic, "let me take you home so that you can rest for a while." So we went home and had some tea, and then I put her to bed.

That evening Isabella stayed in bed, wanting no supper and all the while making plans to go to school the following day. When I suggested that she stay home the next day, she said that she would get a good night's rest, and in the morning she would be okay to go to school.

# Chapter Twelve

## Unscheduled Hospital Visit

The next morning Peter was off to school by himself, as Isabella was still asleep. I went to the farthest corner of the house to make sure that she did not hear my conversation with the doctor at Vancouver Children's Hospital.

As soon as I explained the situation, without a moment of hesitation, he said to me, "Bring her in as soon as possible." The moment she woke up, I told her that we were going to see the doctor at the clinic, even though it was not yet time for her transfusion.

Driving down our regular route to the hospital, at Fifty-ninth and Granville Street in Vancouver, I admired the splendor of the magnolia trees and cherry blossoms. I gasped at the sight of their beauty and tried to distract Isabella by pointing them out to her as well and encouraging her to enjoy the view.

It was the eighth of May when she entered the hospital for the very last time and our life as we knew it changed forever.

Years later, I discovered that this date was also chosen to be Thalassemia Awareness Day. Now, is this a coincidence? Maybe, but I like to think that maybe, just maybe, Isabella may have had something to do with this particular date.

I parked the car in the hospital parking lot as I had done so many other times before, and as we walked toward the clinic, I noticed she could not keep up with me. We had to stop a few times so that she could catch her breath. When we finally made it inside the building, Dr. Smith immediately called us into his office to examine her.

The regular staff and nurses were surprised to see us because only a few days had gone by since her last regular blood transfusion, but as usual, they were warm and friendly. They quickly realized what was going on, so they kept Isabella company while Dr. Smith spoke to me in his office.

The doctor's words were carefully chosen. This was one of those moments that imprinted in my mind and could never be forgotten. He said, "The day that we all feared would come is here. Isabella has gone into heart failure. She won't be going home today. I'm making arrangements to keep her in the hospital."

Outside the room, the nurses were chatting more than usual with Isabella, because the hospital's quarterly magazine was circulating, and my daughter was featured in one of the articles with information on the rare genetic disorder thalassemia. The publication was released on April 16, and Isabella was admitted into the hospital on May 8, just days after celebrating Pat's forty-second birthday.

We had spent his birthday visiting pavilions at Vancouver's memorable 1986 Expo. It was supposed to be a period of celebration for all of us. Before Expo '86 was open, the entire family had passes for the duration of the exposition.

We had all been anxiously waiting to celebrate the summer in the beautiful city that we all loved so much. But the first day we went as a family became more of a problem, because of all the walking; Isabella had to stop frequently and catch her breath. I thought that was strange because she had just been transfused a few days prior. In the past after a transfusion, she would be bursting with energy, but this time she had difficulty keeping up with us. I was totally unprepared for what was happening, even though we knew of the severity of her disease. We were not aware that she was going into cardiac arrest. When Dr. Smith admitted her to the children's hospital, her heart was in really bad shape.

Sadly, by the end of the day at Expo '86, the celebratory feelings had disappeared. We were never able to go back to the Expo sights until after Isabella's death, at which time we felt such grief that we could barely function. So deep was our grief that on a day when we finally mustered enough courage and energy to go, we were not paying attention and were served with two parking tickets.

I had not kept a journal of the daily events and experiences throughout the years that Isabella was physically with us on this earth, but some particular events a mother never forget. The following event is one of them.

After Isabella was settled in her room and the nurses had made her as comfortable as they possibly could, I left her room to get us some lunch in the cafeteria that I knew so well.

In the elevator, I met the doctor from the endocrine clinic with whom we had spent many hours asking questions, assessing Isabella's progress, and monitoring her growth before a decision would be made to induce her with growth hormones. Months had passed since all of the tests had been done, but we never heard whether a decision had been made.

However, as soon as we came face-to-face in the elevator, he recognized me and quickly told me that a decision had been reached to start treating Isabella and that he would proceed as soon as I could make an appointment with his secretary.

I always trusted and respected the decisions of the professionals. I felt that as long as I was the best mother I could possibly be for Isabella, I would leave the health care issues in the capable hands of her doctors, for my own peace of mind, or it would drive me insane.

I convinced myself that the doctor was only doing his job and that protocol had to be followed, but at that moment when he told me that Isabella finally did fit the profile to be treated, I was overcome by anger. I wanted to lash out at him. Again, I felt the injustice and imbalance of our medical system. But all that could come out of my mouth was, "It is too late now; the treatment will no longer be necessary. She has just been admitted to the hospital with congenital heart failure." He was stunned by the news and promised he would come in and see her anyway.

The days that followed were extremely uncomfortable for Isabella. Since her heart was not pumping properly, she retained so much fluid, and her abdomen was extremely bloated. She tried to make light of her condition and used to come up with comments like, "I think I may be having twins!" She was trying to make me feel better by reassuring me with her humor, but we both knew how serious the situation was.

Once again, nothing could prepare us for the next chain of events. Isabella's heart was weak; therefore, we were limited to which drugs could be administered to make her feel better. Sleeping was impossible.

When night came, it was frightening. There was such an eerie feeling in the air; I became sad and lonely as soon as night fell. These feelings still resurface at times when something out of the ordinary is happening around me. Particularly on those occasions, I need to remind myself to be thankful for the day and not allow my mind to go back to those almost unbearable nights of the past.

We would play games to help her sleep, such as visualizing us on the beach of Waikiki, where we had spent such glorious days just a few months earlier. We imagined the waves slapping on the shore, and we would say, "Oh yes, look at that bird resting on the water!" or, "Watch out for the next huge wave!" We continued until it felt like we were actually there and eventually got some rest.

On one of Isabella's weekend outings, when her condition was somewhat stable, we baked cakes, with numerous rest breaks in between. We both delivered them to close friends and relatives who had come to visit her in the hospital. If they were not home, we simply left them at their front door with a note. This was her special way of saying thank you. I had to move fast because she quickly got tired and had to go back to bed to rest.

Isabella returned to the hospital each Monday, and for days after, her trays of food were left untouched. From time to time she would just ask for a slice of toast with butter. Isabella's appetite was poor, and over the years we had nurtured the habit of a well-balanced diet—the rainbow diet as my son calls it today, because the meals always included all the essential food groups. I expressed my concerns to Dr. Smith about her eating toast and butter.

His answer was, "Give her anything she wants. At this point, we don't want to deprive her of anything. Besides, it would not make much difference now, anyway." He knew that I did not want to face the inevitable—that Isabella was at the end of her life.

At least we had the good fortune of being in one of the newest, most well-equipped hospitals in Canada. Isabella was quite excited at the opening ceremonies that took place, as she was one of the first patients to be treated there.

The facilities were wonderful; the staff members were always helpful, with the exception of a few nurses who were not as accommodating as the rest. We soon became well aware of who they were, and when their shift began we would often say, "She must be having a bad day."

Almost a month went by, and Isabella spent Mother's Day in the hospital, but she was determined to acknowledge my birthday at the beginning of June. Imagine my surprise on the morning of my birthday as I entered Isabella's room and saw her face beam with excitement. She wore a smile from ear to ear from the pleasure of being able to complete my birthday card at 3:00 a.m. with hospital construction paper and medical tape. This was a big accomplishment for her.

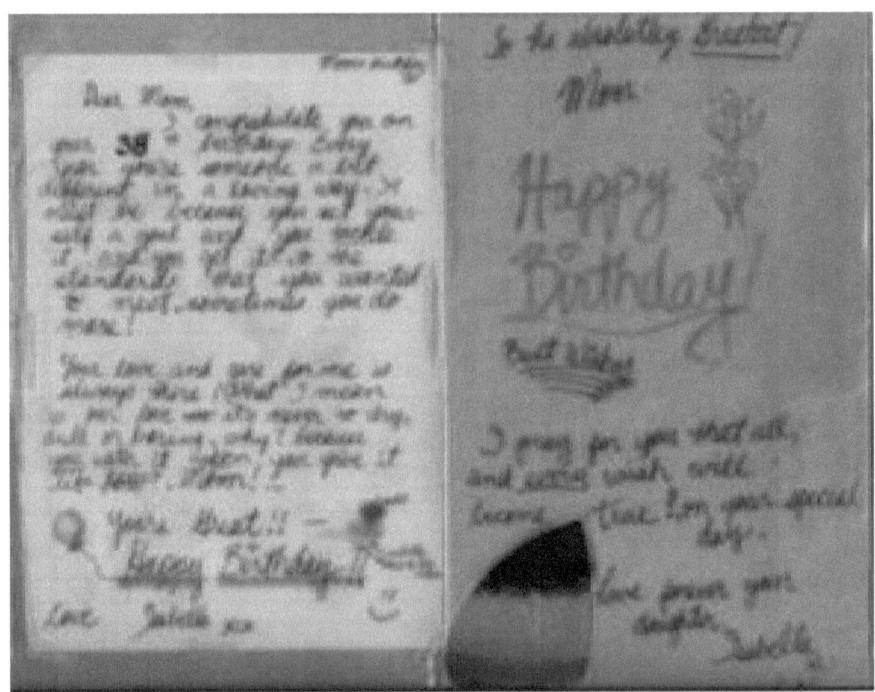

*The last card Isabella made was completed during the night from her hospital bed just in time for her mother's 38th birthday.*

The details of that birthday card were so amazing that it took my breath away. With tears in our eyes and a big, long, affectionate hug, Isabella proceeded to point out to me the details of the card. It included Canadian and American prices, as if it were store bought. The card featured drawings of a colorful and carefully wrapped bouquet of flowers, a bottle of sparkling champagne, and different-colored balloons. It read, "Happy 38th Birthday, Mom." But the hand-written words inside are what touched my heart the most—the words so eloquently chosen to express not only her love for me, but the relationship we both cherished. This was to be my last birthday card from my precious daughter.

In part, the card read:

*Dear Mom, I congratulate you on your 38th birthday. Every year you're someone a bit different in a loving way. It must be because you set yourself a goal and you tackle it and you get it to the standards that you wanted to meet, sometimes you do more!*

*Your love and care for me is always there! What I mean is, our love it's never dry, dull or boring, why? Because you water it often, you give it life, Mom!*

I thank God every day, because my son Peter continues to give me the same thoughtful cards with specially chosen words, at times when I most need them. I also appreciate the insightful messages in his published books that inspire me as well as many others.

The last few weeks that preceded Isabella's passing on to the other side continued to be extremely painful for everyone. Peter, being only three months away from his seventeenth birthday, was by himself or with his school friends much of the time. He found it difficult to visit her at the hospital, seeing her in such pain and not knowing what to do or say. He couldn't protect her now the way he used to at school. But when he did come to visit her, Isabella was always so happy to see him.

There were so many special things that they shared. One late evening at about eleven o'clock, Peter showed up with her favorite McDonald's meal, including french fries. She quickly ditched the hospital food that was still in her room untouched.

For Pat it was also difficult because he wanted to be with Isabella, but, as the sole provider, he needed to continue working. Being self-employed meant that if he did not work, there was no income.

We had already cashed in the children's university funds that were set up at the time of their birth. We did this at a time when we were in great need of extra cash to be able to buy Desferal, the iron-chelating drug. It was a difficult decision, but we were left with no other choice.

With the help of our dedicated doctor and the social worker, who both went beyond their call of duty, we spent a great deal of time and effort writing countless letters to various government and medical officials. We all did everything in our power to lobby to get this new drug covered by Medicare.

# Chapter Thirteen

## *Preparing for the Inevitable*

Even though the many possible complications were clearly explained to us many years before, we still could not believe that the time had come. Isabella was two months away from her fifteenth birthday. We always hoped that one day a cure could be found. But when we were told that she may not have much longer to live, reality began to set in, and we were all in shock.

Phone calls were coming in from family and friends, near and far. So, it was decided to hold a family meeting and figure out how we were going to do the things that needed to be done. We all came together at my younger sister's house, and everyone was given a task. We made a schedule of who was going to stay with Isabella so that Pat and I could take a break.

Other matters needed attending to as well, such as who would get groceries and keep the house ready for us for when Isabella was given day passes to spend at home. One of my neighbors also wanted to know how she could help. "I will do anything," she said.

I replied, "It would be very nice to have the house clean and tidy for Isabella when she comes home this weekend." And she said, "Don't say another word; I will take care of it." She went over and vacuumed, dusted, and scrubbed the bathroom. I will never forget that. I was beyond caring about my pride.

We were by Isabella's bedside around the clock and could not leave her. One Sunday afternoon, the same neighbor who offered to clean my house came up to the hospital with her husband. They brought a picnic basket that included a bottle of wine, and we had a quiet dinner on the beautiful patio located on the hospital's rooftop.

Those were treasured moments that we shared with Isabella amid all the chaos. Some so many other wonderful people were so helpful, such as family members, friends, doctors, nurses, and volunteers who helped make the days just a little brighter.

Isabella had her favorite volunteer. She took a particular liking to this wonderful lady: a mother with four children of her own. She had natural warmth and so much love to give. She would sit and read to Isabella or just chat. She was the only volunteer that Isabella truly enjoyed spending time with, and I felt perfectly comfortable leaving and taking a break now and then.

The help came from all directions, as though it were orchestrated by divine order. It was so well organized, without any effort; everything that needed to be done fell into place effortlessly.

Take for example the visit from Isabella's godmother from Montreal. Mariantonia came at a time when I needed her. She took on the role of the godmother. She was truly a godsend. Her support was so much needed and appreciated, just like that very first day, fourteen and a half years ago, when I was told of Isabella's condition. Mariantonia was the first person I had called to come and stay with me. Ironically, now at the end of Isabella's life, here was Mariantonia, flying from the East Coast to the West Coast to be with us once again.

Even with all the help, it was difficult to watch Isabella suffer through her treatment. The medication given to lessen her physical pain had to be carefully balanced so that it would not interfere with her already overworked heart. Too much medication would cause more harm.

There was also the constant poking of needles for different tests that were needed. It was evident that her heart was not functioning well. We had exhausted all of our options, so we had nothing to lose when we tried a new experimental procedure—administering high doses of Desferal intravenously.

This would mean more pokes and probes. One way of reducing the pokes was to surgically insert a catheter underneath the skin connected to the main heart valve with high doses of iron chelation, in the hope that it would extract enough iron from the heart muscle and reverse the heart condition she was facing. This medical procedure proved to be a real challenge to get approved by the hospital board, because (although not spoken in so many words but understood) this was a waste of time and money from the administration's point of view, due to the low possibility of success; Isabella would die anyway!

But from the parents' viewpoint, we wanted to exhaust all of our options and try anything and everything. Again, I commend our doctors for going to bat for us; they were just as eager as we were to try everything within their power. The final decision was that if the administration would not give the okay, the surgeon would use the free sample he had in his office and go ahead with the procedure, which is exactly what he did.

If this experiment worked, we would see the results in two to three weeks. The Desferal was administered in a direct line to the heart. It had to be mixed with just the right amount of saline or else it would cause a stinging sensation in her veins throughout her system. After careful calculation, the right dose was found. This went on for three weeks, twenty-four hours a day, seven days a week.

Pat and I were by her side at all times. She also knew exactly how many drops per minute were to be administered.

One night a new nurse came in to check the IV and tried to adjust it. Within seconds Isabella noticed the difference and started to scream in agony.

The drip had been accidentally increased. Had it not been adjusted in time, it might have been dangerously close to killing her. After that incident, we never took our eyes off the drip any time it was adjusted.

The waiting period to see if this treatment would work was long and painful. As we anxiously awaited the end of the three weeks, we soon discovered the disheartening results: there was no improvement. And, as a matter of fact, it had further weakened Isabella, physically and emotionally.

This procedure was later tried with other thalassemia patients who were in better health. The objective was to administer high doses of Desferal at the same time they were transfused. The experiment was to see if it would reduce the iron accumulation in their major organs.

Isabella's heart and other major organs were too damaged by the iron accumulation, and it did not work for her. This procedure was continued for other thalassemia patients for a few years but was later abandoned when no positive results were noted.

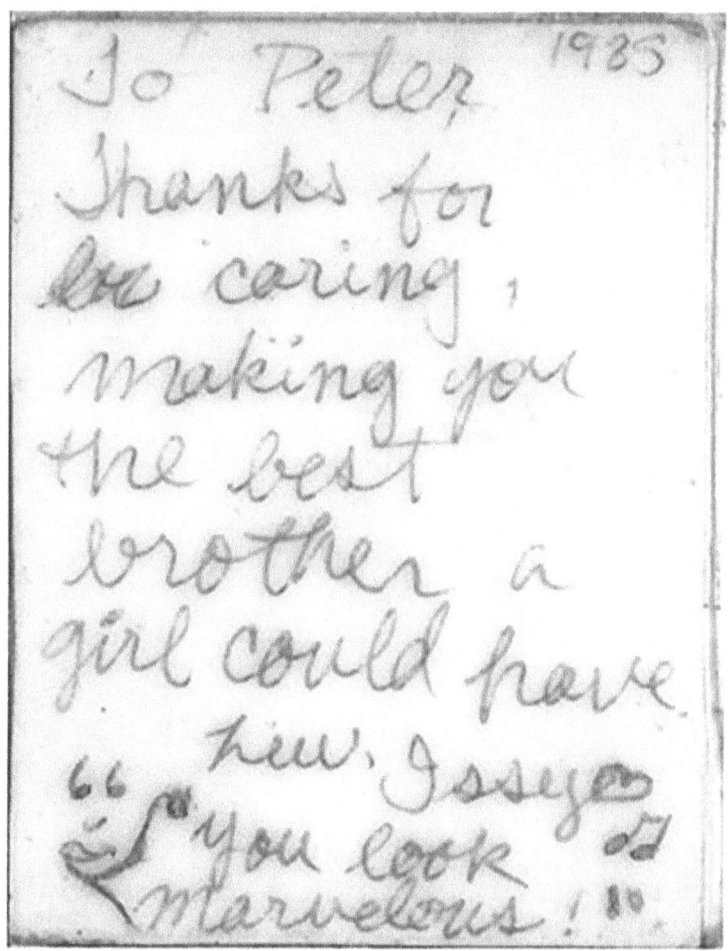

*Isabella's photo to brother Peter, with a special note on the back.*

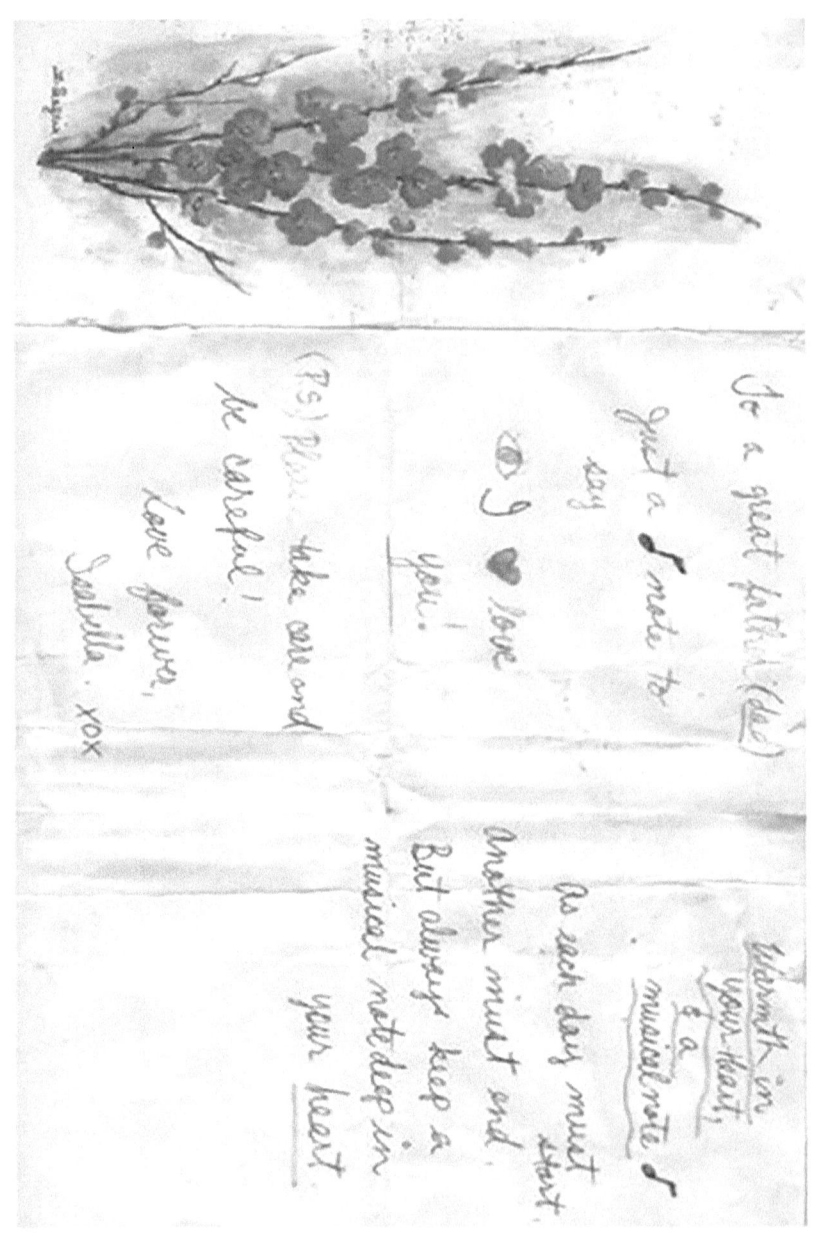

*A special note to Dad from Isabella*

# Chapter Fourteen

## *Special Visitors*

The end of Isabella's life was imminent. A stream of visitors kept on coming and leaving with heavy hearts. One of the visits was from a particular teacher who went above and beyond his duty, and I thought it very kind of him. After a few minutes in the room making small talk, Isabella noticed his discomfort at seeing her in such a disheartening medical condition. She looked so different from the vibrant and cheerful young lady he was used to seeing in his classroom.

Isabella turned to me and said, "Mom, why don't you show Mr. Jones around, and I will take a nap." At the end of the visit when we were alone again, I asked why she wanted me to show him around. "He came to visit you, not the hospital," I said. She quietly replied, "Yes, I know, Mom, but didn't you see how uncomfortable he was?"

Even as sick as she was, she always managed to place others before herself. That's just the kind of person she was, and I drew from that strength. Yet she always tried her best to fit in and be like everyone else. Looking at her, it appeared there was nothing wrong, but the complexity of her illness was not understood by most.

Her room at the hospital had double doors, and both doors were kept closed. This setup served to be very helpful during the times when she was in so much pain that her screams would carry down the corridors were it not for those doors.

One day, a few weeks after her funeral, I was visiting the ward where she had spent her last three months. I wanted to visit because I still felt the connection with her there and also had made friends with so many of the patients, their families, and staff. On this particular occasion, I saw one mother whose son I knew was suffering from a form of cancer.

She stopped me in the hallway and said, "I feel I owe you an apology." I inquired, "What for?" She proceeded to explain that she felt guilty about her envious thoughts, seeing Isabella and me in the hospital and wondering how seriously ill she could be. This mother had thought, "She doesn't have cancer; she has all of her hair, unlike my son." We chatted for a while, and then she was happy to tell me that her son was now in remission and things were looking well. Very promising for him, but my daughter had passed on.

She felt guilty and wanted to share this with me. I assured her that she was not the only person who had harbored those thoughts, and I wished her and her son and family all the best.

One of the few happy memories during Isabella's hospital stay was the wish granted to her by the wonderful Make-A-Wish Foundation. Our family were avid fans of the show Family Ties, starring Michael J. Fox. Isabella identified herself with the famous character Alex, partly because his character was so witty and cute, but also because he was small in stature like her.

When the Make-A-Wish Foundation asked what her wish would be, and they would try their best to honor it, she asked if she could have lunch with or just meet her favorite actor, Michael J. Fox. She was told that they would do their best to fulfill her wish. Regrettably, at the time, Michael was filming Back to the Future in New York; therefore, it would be impossible to arrange, as Isabella was not in any condition to travel. However, she was promised that he would contact her by phone and have a little chat with her. She was so excited about that prospect.

The hospital phone rang one day, and, sure enough, it was *the* phone call she had been anxiously waiting for. But the pain was so intense that now she had no energy to talk and asked if he would call back when she felt better. True to his word, he did call back a few days later.

This time she prepared herself like a typical teenager, lying on the bed and holding the telephone with her free hand. For one moment I pictured her talking to an old friend as she used to; but when she tried to say something, she simply did not have enough breath left in her except to say how sorry she was that she could not talk to him. On his third try, it was too late.

I commend Michael, such a popular actor, even though none of his fans knew about his medical condition at that time. Isabella had surely picked a winner in terms of a caring humanitarian. As we now know, Michael J Fox is a very special individual; Isabella knew it then. For him to take the time from his busy schedule to grant a dying wish to a young girl—it was truly special. Thank you, Michael.

The Make-A-Wish Foundation wanted to do more for us because Isabella's wish was only partly granted; therefore, a complimentary lunch was offered to Pat, Peter, and me, at a restaurant of our choice. Weeks after the funeral, when our heads felt somewhat clearer, the three of us had lunch at a unique Japanese restaurant in honor of Isabella. I still sense the bittersweet experience of that lunch in every inch of my body. On one hand, it was a treat to have a meal in such an exclusive restaurant, with its scrumptious food; but, on the other hand, all three of us kept looking at the empty chair where Isabella would be sitting if she were alive.

During the last few weeks of Isabella's life, when there was no other hope but to make her feel as comfortable as possible, on weekends she was sent home. Meanwhile, her body was slowly shutting down. She was constantly on a portable oxygen tank to help with her breathing, and in a wheelchair to help her to get around, because her little body was so swollen, her legs twice their normal size from water retention.

However, at times she would still venture out on her own, sliding down the flight of stairs in our family home, slowly, one step at a time. Getting back up the stairs again was impossible, because, first of all, she couldn't bend her legs, and second, she would quickly run out of breath.

That's when big brother Peter would come to the rescue by carrying her in his arms and putting her either back in her new waterbed that her dad had bought with hopes that she would sleep more comfortably, or in her favorite chair, where she spent her very last night talking with her brother.

# *Chapter Fifteen*

## *Our Last Farewell*

The morning after that talk, it was obvious what was happening, so the ambulance was called. Isabella waved at Peter, and he stood there waving back at us as the ambulance sped off into the morning rush-hour traffic. That was the last time he was to see her alive. It was Monday, July 28, 1986.

As the ambulance arrived at the hospital, we were quickly greeted by nurses and attending physicians as they began working on Isabella with lightning speed, or so it seemed to me. There was no time to lose. Her body was completely shutting down. At this point, she had shed all of her inhibition. It didn't matter anymore what they were doing to her body. She was in and out of consciousness. As soon as she was stabilized, she was brought up to her usual room in ward 3B.

Morphine was administered, only now we were no longer concerned if it interfered with her heart function. All that we were aiming for was for her to be comfortable until the angels came for her.

Isabella would wake up every so often and talk with us, completely aware of her surroundings as she spoke with clarity about whatever was on her mind.

The family was gathered around. She heard us whispering and asked who had died. To our surprise, she had overheard us discussing my grandmother, Serafina, whom I was named after. Serafina had just passed away that morning in another city, and funeral arrangements were being made.

All the family members came to say their last goodbyes to Isabella. As one of them entered the room and approached her, Isabella noticed a Band-Aid on her arm. The relative explained that she had just had a blood test. Without any hesitation, Isabella asked her, "So are you pregnant?"

She answered, "I don't know yet; I'm waiting for the test results." It turned out she was pregnant with her second child.

Isabella was also experiencing some hallucinations that the medical staff dismissed as due to the drugs. But for the first time in months, Isabella was like herself again. She had a calm, peaceful look on her face.

She woke up from time to time and told us that she had been visited by different people whom we never saw in the room, such as a beautiful lady dressed in a long blue gown. "Did you see her?" she would ask. One could say it was a hallucination, but I suspect it was not.

That night, for the first time since Isabella entered the hospital, I took advantage of using what the hospital called "the quiet room" to sleep. Mariantonia, her godmother, stayed in the room with her during the night before catching her morning flight back home to Montreal. Eventually, the rest of the family left. Pat was also encouraged to go home and stay with Peter; plus, he had work to do and the family business to run.

That evening I surrendered and asked God to do whatever was best for my daughter. I could not bear to see her suffer any longer. I was ready to let her go! That night I had the most restful night in months. Isabella had a peaceful night as well, I learned from Mariantonia, who had been by her bedside.

Mary and I said our goodbyes, and she left the hospital. I watched Isabella coming in and out of consciousness until mid-morning on Tuesday, July 29. Pat had decided not to go to work. I was hoping and waiting anxiously for him to come to the hospital and be by her side as well.

My gut feeling told me that there was very little time left and that it would be a matter of minutes before she would slip away from us forever. It was as if she knew too and was waiting until her father arrived. At ten o'clock her hospital door opened; it was Pat, just arriving.

While his hand was still on the doorknob, Isabella opened her eyes, took a long look at her father, and then gently smiled her famous smile. No words were necessary. One single teardrop ran down the left side of her face as she took her last breath.

I remember clearly what took place in the hospital room that morning, right down to what I wore (my pink V-neck sweater and pink pants). In sheer desperation, I fell to my knees and let out a loud scream. Tears ran down my face, where they had been absent all this time. I had not allowed myself to cry before, for fear I would never be able to stop. But now it was like a faucet that had suddenly been turned on, and I could not shut it off.

My heart felt as if it was breaking, and there was nothing I could do about it. I was no longer in control of my emotions, as I had managed to be for the last fourteen years. A part of me was gone forever with Isabella. She was now in God's arms, to guide us all from heaven because her work here on earth was completed.

Nothing in this world could have possibly prepared me for this moment. I had shed no tears until now because I had always kept hoping and praying that things could change. But the heroic persona that I had tried to portray suddenly left me.

Pat and I had always taken turns consoling each other. When one of us was down, the other would take over and be strong. At this moment, I felt his strength, and I knew that together we would make it through.

Peter reacted bravely to Isabella's death. When Peter was a teen, it was hard at times to know the best way to deal with him. Sometimes he put up a tough and indifferent front, but that was exactly what it was, a front. Pat and I had each other, but he had lost his most trusted support system, his only sibling, his sister. She would no longer be able to give him a tongue-lashing when, somehow, she always managed to win the verbal arguments between the two of them.

I'm not sure what happened after Isabella passed. Suddenly I felt as if I were in a fog, with everything moving in slow motion. My body and mind seemed to have shifted to autopilot. I remember family members arriving one by one, in silence. Then we all wept, and each of us started our own grieving process.

Finally, I don't know what came over me. I told everyone that it was time for all of us to go; we had arrangements to make.

Peter, however, did not want to leave the room and asked if he could spend some time alone with Isabella. He wanted to bid farewell to her in private. Their connection was unique and much deeper than with any other siblings I have ever known. He had felt and experienced her passing the very moment it happened, even before anyone had given him the news. He was still at the family home, as he had refused to drive to the hospital with his father.

One of Peter's aunts had gone to the house to give him the news and asked him what he was doing still at home. "Don't you know your sister just died?" she asked. He flatly replied, "I know already." She asked again how he knew and who had told him. He replied again, "I just know."

When his aunt offered to drive him to the hospital, he declined the offer (not too graciously, I might add) and insisted on driving himself. Peter drove himself, speeding, to the hospital and was pulled over by a police officer. He was, after all, a new driver. When Peter was asked by the officer why he insisted on speeding, he said it was because his sister had died. The officer told him that was all the more reason why he should not be driving at all. The speeding continued for the next few months until his license was suspended. The suspension was a blessing, even though he did not think so at the time. It gave him a chance to reflect on what had just happened.

Peter eventually got to the hospital and spent the time alone with Isabella in silence, as he had requested. The lengthy conversations had already taken place two nights prior, and what needed to be said between them had already been said.

# Chapter Sixteen

*The Grieving Process*

As we filed out of the hospital room and headed for the parking lot, I couldn't help but notice the beautiful blue summer sky and the sun shining brightly. I thought, "How can this be? How can people be talking and walking? Don't they know that my world has just fallen apart?"

As we approached our car, we were asked who was driving us home. Pat answered calmly, "I will drive home." He said to this dear friend, "She is not with us physically, but she is still present here with her vibration. Everything is vibrational." This concept was unheard of by many and not accepted by most.

Later that evening, the three of us—Pat, Peter, and I— lay on our backs outside Isabella's bedroom door across from Peter's room, reminiscing and talking for a very long time. When Peter was asked how he had known that Isabella had passed on, even though no one had yet called him, he said he had felt it. He felt her presence there with him at the very same time she took her last breath.

Tania and Tiger were our pet cats. Tania, Isabella's cat, was on Peter's bed. She suddenly looked up as if she had seen something up near the ceiling, then leaped off the bed. It has been said that pets can see and sense so much more than we can. Was Tania seeing something in the room not visible to the human eye? We will never know for sure. But the timing of the cat's reaction seemed to be more than just coincidental.

There was nothing left to do now but to make funeral arrangements. Even though it was a modest funeral, it was hard to miss the sea of flowers sent from across Canada and from Europe. As most families usually request that, in lieu of flowers, donations may be made to a favorite organization, we had asked that donations be sent to the children's hospital for thalassemia research. Since there was no local thalassemia research being conducted at the time, the hospital placed the funds in a special account, and a portion of it was later used to print informational literature on thalassemia. The rest, along with donations from Pat's company, was used to fund the initial registration expenses for the Vancouver Thalassemia Society of British Columbia.

When the funeral mass for Isabella was over and the casket was sealed, Peter pleaded with the funeral director to reopen it so he could have one more look at her face. This was a most unusual request, but seeing the pained look on our son's face, the director agreed and granted his request.

In the car on the way to the cemetery, the three of us were actually able to laugh at some memories we had of Isabella like the way she would roll her eyes when she did not agree with you or some other silly thing. It was the first time in weeks that we had had a good laugh; it was as if a big burden had been lifted, and we realized that we no longer needed to worry about her being in pain ever again.

We needed to hang on to this thought often because we were all faced with the task of somehow accepting that she was no longer physically with us. We needed to remind ourselves that even though we could no longer touch her, her spirit was still very close to us.

I often pictured her coming down the stairs and stopping midway to talk to me as I worked in the kitchen. Sometimes I could almost reach out and touch her but then realized she was not there; it was only my imagination.

These images of her occurred often in many areas of the house, so much so that I started to plead with Pat to move. After much discussion on the topic, we did sell that house, and I'm very happy to say that I love my new home. However, if I had waited a little longer until the images of Isabella were not as vivid, I think I would have preferred to have stayed in that house, where happy and sad memories lived.

Each and every one of us goes through the grieving process in a different way, and our family was no exception. One of my nieces went out and bought an outfit exactly like the one Isabella had worn, thinking it would please me, but it had the opposite effect.

The outfit was particularly special because Isabella had pleaded with me to buy it for her, and when I told her I did not have the extra money to purchase it, she saved up enough from her allowance and paid for it herself. That outfit was a pretty one. She loved it so much that she wore it on every special occasion. It made her look as grown up (more like her real age) on the outside as she felt on the inside. For this reason, when it came time to pick the clothes for the funeral, I knew exactly which one Isabella would choose for her final farewell.

When I saw my niece in that same outfit, I was angry, upset, and sad. I was upset because I felt that she was trying to compare herself with my daughter. Nothing could replace my daughter, and I was sad that it was not my daughter in that outfit. I realize now what my niece was trying to do, and perhaps I ought to have been honored that she tried to imitate her cousin. But to me, it seemed to take away from her memory. Right or wrong, that was the way I felt and consequently reacted.

The days and months that followed were challenging, to say the least. There was such a void in my life. I had to try very hard to even imagine Isabella's sweet face and big smile. I had to remind myself constantly that she was in a better place and that although I could not see her touch her or hear her infectious laughter, she was near me at all times. I had to come to terms with the fact that I would never get to see her graduate or get married and have a family; none of those events would ever take place.

The only thought that would bring me comfort was that she was no longer suffering and that she was happy where she was. Her work here among us was completed. I had to hang on to this idea just to get through each day.

I now had to fill all that empty time that had been previously spent caring for Isabella. I felt that I needed to occupy myself with worthwhile activities. I begged my neighbor for the job she had offered me on the day of Isabella's funeral—when I was ready. I kept reminding her that I was ready. At least I thought I was ready, but obviously, she thought I was crazy because she kept on stalling me. Finally, after pestering her for a long time, I got her to say yes. I thought this was great. It kept me busy, and I earned some money. This lasted only a few months, and I soon realized that this was not what I wanted to do.

# *Chapter Seventeen*

## *Forming a Support Group*

It was time for me to start a support group for families and patients of thalassemia, to bring about the kind of support that I felt was lacking during Isabella's treatment. Being able to get together with other patients and family members to share our stories would help one another out.

I wanted patients, families, and medical professionals to get together and share their concerns and ideas to improve treatment and communication. It was badly needed, because being misunderstood had affected my family and me all of those years.

One of the ways to raise the profile of thalassemia was to educate the public and promote awareness.

During the years that Isabella was treated, I had the opportunity of meeting only a handful of individuals in the same situation, but we were all treated at different times and by different doctors. To get in touch with these patients and their families, I needed to meet them at the hospital while they were getting transfused, introduce myself, tell them what I was planning to do, and exchange telephone numbers.

This meant many frequent trips to the children's hospital on the off-chance that every time I went, I could meet a new patient being treated. This went on for a few months until word got around, and eventually, a date, time, and place were set.

I asked permission from the hospital to place handwritten posters in various areas and waited anxiously at the first meeting to see who would show up. I convinced myself that even if just one showed up, all of my efforts were worth it.

I did not know where to start; I didn't have a clue about how I was going to bring this group together. Grief can be a great motivator; I kept on reminding myself that if I could survive the death of my daughter, I could do anything I set my mind to do. I was unstoppable and forged on by going to the children's hospital every time I thought there might be a patient with thalassemia and communicating to them what I was trying to do. Everyone that I had a chance to talk to was very excited. The word spread quickly.

Soon we began meeting on a regular monthly basis. To be taken seriously and to proceed with our goal, we needed to give this group a name and be legally registered. That's how the Vancouver Thalassemia Society was formed.

Even though the group was small, the enthusiasm that was generated from these meetings was contagious. We all agreed that we needed to raise awareness of this illness and began targeting the high-risk groups in our community and speaking to ethnic groups at luncheons and other events.

I used the article that was printed only months earlier by the children's hospital and by the Vancouver Sun newspaper to help me explain what thalassemia was, how it impacted families, and how many were not even aware they were carrying this gene.

I was no speaker; I had never spoken in public in my life. Anyone who knows me knows that I'm shy and would rather be that one person in the corner who just observes. What kept me going was the deep desire to help others avoid the same pitfalls I had experienced, and that gave me the strength and commitment to continue.

Our first fundraiser took place at a venue where the owner welcomed us with open arms and gave us permission to use his facilities and anything else we needed. The evening was a success. As soon as I finished explaining my daughter's story and what the society was trying to do, guests kept bringing their donations up to the stage; I had never seen anything like it before. People's hearts and wallets opened up that evening, and the generosity continued at every function at which I spoke.

It was at this time that I had the opportunity to meet some thalassemia carriers who generously donated their time to help out. The accounting books needed to be kept in order so that any funds collected were properly managed.

One particular volunteer, Anastasia, was enormously helpful in taking care of the books, fundraising, and lobbying to establish the same treatment protocols used throughout Europe. Others, too numerous to mention by name volunteered by putting the society by-laws together and, submitting them to the government. Others helped with many other tasks that were essential in forming this group.

My very first knowledge of thalassemia was at the time of Isabella's diagnosis, in 1972. Prior to this time, my husband and I had no clue what thalassemia was or that we were both carriers of this gene. The informal support group that first started in 1986 became a registered society in 1987.

In 1986 a nonprofit, patient organization was formed: the Thalassemia International Federation. In 1996 it joined forces with the World Health Organization. Together these two groups have been instrumental in overseeing the establishment of a treatment protocol for thalassemia. They are the bridge for more than a hundred national thalassemia associations worldwide.

During conferences that are held in different countries, patients and medical professionals come together to share their knowledge and expertise. The first conference that I attended was held in New York in 1990, shortly after the Vancouver Thalassemia Society was established.

It was a trip I could ill afford to take, but Pat, with his big, generous heart, saw how important it was for me; he gave his blessing and paid for all of the expenses so that I could attend. I returned home with an enormous amount of enthusiasm and helpful information, which was used to move our new support group in Vancouver forward. For me and for many other individuals who attended this conference, it was the most electrifying, positive experience.

To date, thalassemia is still virtually unheard of, even though it is one of the most common blood disorders in the world. One of the reasons is that a carrier of the gene could live a perfectly normal life, unaware of thalassemia unless his or her partner is also a carrier and they have children that inherit the affected gene from both parents. Another reason for ignorance may be that certain cultures do not want to talk about thalassemia.

So, until this thinking is somehow changed, there will always be newborn babies with this condition.

I needed to step back from my close involvement in society, partly because the various cultures and customs are so diverse that it was hard to come together at times, and the common goal was easily lost in the process.

There is so much more to be done. More research on thalassemia and studies on new iron chelation therapy are desperately needed.

Working closely with doctors is the only way to determine what form of iron chelation works best for each patient.

Bone marrow transplant is still the only way to extend life expectancy, for those fortunate enough to receive it. This treatment is not for everyone, because of the enormous complications involved which limits the candidates for the procedure.

The younger the patient is, the more successful the surgery. It is one step closer to a normal lifestyle and will eventually reduce or eradicate this disease altogether.

To identify a carrier of thalassemia, one must ask specific questions, and there is a test called hemoglobin electrophoresis. Testing can also be done during pregnancy to determine whether the baby will be affected, giving the parents a chance to be educated about the facts. Therefore, I cannot stress enough the importance of talking to your doctor and being open to genetic counseling, particularly if one is in the high-risk category.

# Chapter Eighteen

*Continuing On*

My life and the lives of my husband and son have evolved tremendously—for the most part in a positive way—as a result of our experiences. Living with Isabella and knowing that her life would be short has brought us the highest of highs and the lowest of lows. We held on tight to the possibility that a cure could be found during her lifetime; this was constantly on everyone's mind, but this wish never materialized. Nevertheless, this experience has made all three of us more empathetic, it has strengthened us as individuals, and it has given us the courage to do anything that we want to do.

A couple of years after the Vancouver Thalassemia Society was formed and was off and growing, I needed to create some distance to move forward with my life. So, I embarked on a new project that took me back to school. I gained all the qualifications needed for this new career; while maintaining and creating some balance. This was interesting for me because it was so different from anything I had experienced before. It captured my interest for twenty years.

After carefully examining all of the pros and cons and satisfaction of the work I was doing, I came to realize that the experience paled in comparison to that of being a mother. It confirmed that my job as a mother was without a doubt the most rewarding for me.

My firm belief in a higher power has always helped me overcome difficult situations. I thank God every day for giving me the opportunity to serve Him as I did. He has given me the guidance to instill strong values in my son, Peter, during many years of turmoil and deep sadness, and the wisdom to encourage him to be or do whatever he chooses to do.

There is no question that during the early years of childhood, my main concern was Isabella, because of her ongoing health challenges. Though I was equipped with all of the best intentions to be fair to both of my children, I can't help but wonder if, at times, I unintentionally neglected Peter's needs— even though he has never given any indication of resentment or neglect.

From a very young age, Peter always seemed to be wiser than his years. He understood the severity of Isabella's condition and that she required constant care. Years later, now that we are both adults, our bond is stronger than ever.

We remain very close, all the while respecting each other's choices. His tremendous insight and empathy for others leave me breathless.

After Isabella's death, I was very well aware that despite his youthful wisdom, Peter still needed guidance, because he was, after all, only seventeen years old. There were plenty of opportunities and reasons for Peter to make all the wrong choices. But he did not disappoint me and instead impressed me with the good company he kept. He hung out with the right crowds and made the right choices, such as being involved in sports. Soccer was his passion, and he kept fit as well by going to the gym regularly. This made me very happy because it kept him involved in a healthy lifestyle and away from trouble.

Peter's friends were from a variety of different backgrounds. This was evident when, at the time of the funeral preparation, I wanted him to participate in the arrangements. Pat and I asked him to pick six friends to be the pallbearers. So unique were the individuals that he chose, that it looked more like the United Nations coming together at a memorial ceremony.

As an adult, Peter has proven to be an accomplished author and has a career in conflict resolution. He is a life coach and spiritual adviser. But more important than his accomplishments is his warm heart. He is a kind human being with an exciting future ahead of him.

My longing to be surrounded by a large family, including grandchildren, is still very much alive. I have such happy memories of my parents' celebrations with all of their children and numerous grandchildren, especially during the holiday time. For compensation, I have been truly blessed with so many good friends whom I can always call on for anything. What more can anyone ask? I feel so fortunate.

My husband, Pat, remains the love of my life. We have been happily married for over forty years. Our relationship has sustained many bumps in the road. We have had to carefully choose our battles, but I'm happy to say that we have come out stronger than ever.

Pat is, and always will be, my rock. At times I have those hysterical moments that are typical to many women, but his calm approach to problem-solving quickly grounds me. I continue to count on his love and support. I admire the way he has maintained his sense of humor, even with so many losses in his life—the loss of our daughter, the sudden and tragic loss of his younger brother, Frank, whom he was particularly close to, and the loss of his parents. These experiences forced Pat to become responsible at a very young age because there were so many people around him who needed his guidance; hence, I can always count on his wisdom.

Pat's positive outlook and zest for life are beyond words. His sense of responsibility as a family man has never wavered. Always wise and hardworking, he is a man who left his hometown at an early age to venture to a new country in an effort to make a better life for himself and his family. Pat was the eldest of four boys, and because his father was in poor health, he took on the responsibility of a man at a very young age.

Now in his golden years, Pat continues to work hard and run a business, winning numerous awards for his excellent craftsmanship.

Dedicated to being a good provider and running his business with integrity, Pat is honest and trustworthy, but most of all, a warm and gentle man.

I feel very fortunate for what I have. Yes, we have had our share of hard financial times as well, but those are the bumps in the road for most people on this planet. This is part of the experience in the school of life.

My belief is that when we are faced with difficult times (and we all are, at one time or another), what counts is how we get back on track again and get on with the business of living. Over the years, during times of trial, I felt I was being truly tested, but I never lost sight of what I had, and I realized that there is always someone less fortunate.

I really believe that if we would all stop once in a while to count our blessings, we would have no time left for complaints. This has and always will be my philosophy; it has carried me through some rough days.

Some of Isabella's friends who knew her well said that she would always be remembered for her happy face and especially for her laugh that would cheer anyone up. Although Isabella endured many problems, she never let on that she was in pain; she was always concerned about everybody else and their problems.

She knew her life was to be short but got the most out of it by living each day to the fullest.

Isabella had dreams just like her friends, and even though she did not get to fulfill them all, she left us behind something to admire and respect—her life and the way she lived it.

# *Chapter Nineteen*

## *My Thoughts on Thalassemia*

I would like to see a worldwide campaign to educate people about thalassemia and its impact on families. I would also like equal rights for patients trying to access treatment and services.

The various levels and conditions of the disorder make it difficult to diagnose and treat properly. We need more research to find more effective and less invasive methods of iron chelation than Desferal.

There is still a lack of knowledge about thalassemia among the general public, and to some extent, the medical profession. One of the reasons we don't hear much about thalassemia is that many families directly affected do not wish to talk about it.

Some cultures may consider it a stigma and may not want to feel alienated or ashamed of this inherited disease. Without an informed community, the affected individuals feel alone, isolated, and misunderstood.

Genetic counseling and testing should be made mandatory, especially for high-risk groups. Young people who carry the thalassemia gene, especially those planning a family, need to be aware of the risks and then make their own decisions, but we need to give people choices.

Thalassemia is affecting families throughout the world, children are dying from it every day, and yet few people know about it. This has to change; we owe it to our future generations and their well-being. Children with thalassemia cannot fight for themselves; it is up to us, and it is our duty, to become the ambassadors for a better life for innocent children.

Therefore, I urge you—if you suspect that you may be a carrier of thalassemia, please take the test and find out for sure. It is just a simple blood test. If you find out that you are a carrier of this gene, this knowledge will only empower you.

May your journey be a blessed one, filled with joy and good health.

## Here I Sit—
## A Burden

I hardly move and I can't fetch for myself.
Here I am, I sit a burden,
To have so many aches and pains, but Inside
of me, lies the most pain.

I seem to do nothing but groan and complain.
Some is shared with Dad, but too much is given to my Mother.

Here and there, mainly here, I sit a burden.
I say not much, I don't wish to take a call from someone, Many
times not even a friend.
Here I sit a burden; will this ever end?

I feel for a friend, but it no longer is the same.
I can barely relate, many find it hard to face me When
I'm in pain or not looking so great.

So many find they try to speak, but they always seem
Scared that they might say something to hurt me,
Or upset me; what they think is that I am weak and
Have to be treated so very sweetly.

You might think this is new and that I have never felt it before; no,
because I have felt it in the past.

Only now it may be worse, this may change. But not now, not soon, not soon at all.

*Written by Isabella Sammarco*
*July 2, 1986 (days before her passing)*

The following poems were printed in the high school yearbook by some of Isabella's closest friends.

## Isabella Sammarco

Farewell, my friend, the time has come
To say our last goodbye;
You've loved and laughed these many months While
I, alone, have cried.

Hope you've had much happiness in life
And though your dusk is near,
I hope before your lifetime fades
You'll learn to shed a tear.

All these long years you've given free,
Few tokens you have asked for;
And now as darkness beckons me
You give and then you give more.

That girlish charm you hide behind,
It dazzles all who see,
But I, best friend, have cracked the mask
And faced reality.

Near fifteen years you've walked this earth,
How hard a life you've lived;
And still although you've hated to take, You
always thought to give.

By Lisa Lee

## Gone

The moon shines upon water
Reflecting days gone by.
Memories of you slowly
                    Slow
                    ly
                    Slow
                    ly
                    Slipping
                    away, Into
                    gray.

Wild dogs, I hear,
Baying at a distant moon;
I see as they do.
A moon that is gone,
Just like you,
Covered by clouds.

They bring back memories of you.
Now gone,
Somewhere in the past?
                    Future?
                    Distanc
                    e?

Gone, somewhere,
Gone to peacefulness,
Gone.


By Greg Cooper

You told me the hurting would go away, But
it's there when I wake, every day.

You said you loved me and you always will.
I need you now, there is a space for you to fill. Forever
in my heart, this love will last,
As I look onto the future and back on the past. By


Kirsten McGrath

# Acknowledgments

My deepest appreciation goes to my husband, Pasquale, who has been a constant support in any project that I embark upon; and writing Isabella's memoir was no exception.

Thanks to my son, Peter, for guiding me along the way through each step and continuing to affirm that I can complete this project.

Thanks to Debbie Horne, a longtime friend, who made the excellent suggestion of simply writing for only fifteen minutes, at a time when putting pen to paper seemed much too overwhelming; and this is exactly what I did.

To Valerie O'Connal: for her insight, warm heart, and encouragement, and for putting her tremendous computer expertise to work.

And to Cate Pedersen for her professional and loving guidance in editing my simple notes and allowing my voice to come through as genuinely as it was intended.

I'm grateful to the very talented artist Andrea Autelitano, for his drawings and his willingness to take the time out of his busy schedule to accommodate my requests for any changes that needed to be done.

Many thanks also go to Jessica Douzenis at The Press Room Full Service Printing, for her patience and understanding when putting everything together became too overwhelming for me.

I also wish to express a special thanks to Dr. David F. Smith and his loyal staff, who always helped Isabella to feel at home during every blood transfusion. Dr. Smith was instrumental in achieving the highest-quality care for thalassemia patients by spending endless hours writing letters to various medical departments and government officials.

# Foundations and Resources

**Thalassaemia International Federation**
PO Box 28807
2083
Nicosia
Cyprus

Tel: + 357 22 319 129
Fax: + 357 22 314 552
Email: thalassaemia@cytanet.com.cy

Business hours: 9:00 a.m.–3:00 p.m. (Monday–Friday GMT+2)

All information received, including name, e-mail, phone, and postal address, as well as content (such as personal information, questions, and any data), will not be passed on to any third party and will be used only for the purpose it was sent.

This website does not collect any cookies.

**TIF MEMBER ASSOCIATIONS**

Please note this section contains links only to those member associations that have websites.

**Albania**
Albanian Thalassaemics Association ATA

**Argentina**
Thalassaemia Foundation of Argentina FUNDATAL,
http://www.fundatal.org.ar/

## Australia
Australian Thalassaemia Association, http://www.tsv.org.au/
Thalassaemia Society of New South Wales,
http://www.thalnsw.org.au/
Thalassaemia Australia Inc., www.tsv.org.au

## Azerbaijan
Association Parents of Children with Thalassaemia Savad Dunyasi
Azerbaijan Thalassaemia Society INSAN

## Bahrain
Bahrain National Hereditary Anemia Society

## Bangladesh
Bangladesh Thalassaemia Society
Bangladesh Thalassaemia Foundation, http://www.thals.org/
Thalassaemia Welfare Centre Bangladesh

## Belgium
Association Belge de Thalassémie ASBL,
http://www.abthalassemie.be/
Association Belgo-Mediterranéenne de Lutte Contre la
Thalassemie

## Brazil
Associacao Brasileira dos Thalassaemicos ABRASTA,
http://www.abrasta.org.br/

## Bulgaria
Bulgarian Anti-Thalassaemia Organisation
BATA, http://www.anti-thalassaemia.bg/
Thalassaemics' Organisation in Bulgaria TOB,
http://www.otbulgaria.com/

## Cambodia
Cambodian Thalassaemia Association

## Canada
Thalassaemia Foundation of Canada, http://www.thalassemia.ca/
Vancouver Thalassaemia Society of B.C.

## China
Children's Thalassaemia Foundation Ltd
Thalassaemia Association of Hong Kong,
http://www.thalassaemia.org.hk/

## Cyprus
Pan-Cyprian Antianaemia Association

## Egypt
Egyptian Thalassaemic Friends Association

## France
Association Française de Lutte Contre les
Thalassaemies, http://pagesperso-
orange.fr/aflt/index1.htm

## Germany
Thalassemia Verein Ulm, http://www.thalassaemieverein-ulm.de/
Interessengemeinschaft Sichelzellkrankheit und Thalassaemia e.V.

## Greece
Thalassaemia Federation of Greece,
http://www.thalassaemia.gr/enter.html
Thalassaemia Association Korinthou

## India
Thalassaemics India,
http://www.thalassemicsindia.org/ Federation of
Indian Thalassaemics,
Foundation Against Thalassaemia, http://www.thalassaemia.in/
Indian Association of Blood Cancer & Allied Diseases,
http://www.cancerlifeblood.org/

Mumbai Thalassaemic Society
National Thalassaemia Welfare Society,
http://www.thalassemiaindia.org/
Nivethan Trust, http://www.nivethan.org/
Parents Association Thalassaemic Unit Trust
Research Society of BJW Hospital for
Children Thalassaemia & Sickle Cell Society
of Bombay Thalassaemic Children Welfare
Association
Thalassaemia Society of India

**Indonesia**
Yayasan Thalassaemia Indonesia,
http://www.thalassaemia- yti.or.id/

**Iran**
Charity Foundation for Special Diseases, http://www.cffsd.org/
Iranian Thalassaemia Society, http://iranianthalassemia.com/
Esfahan Thalassaemia Society

**Iraq**
Ninava Thalassaemia Society, Mosul, http://www.ninavasemia.
blogspot.com/
Iraqi Thalassaemia Association

**Israel**
Israeli Association of Thalassaemia & Sickle Cell Anemia

**Italy**
Association Veneta per la Lotta alla Talassemia (AVLT),
http://www.avlt.it/
Associazione Talassemici e Drepanocity Lombardi ONLUS
Fondazione Italiana "L. Giambrone" per la Guarigione dalla
Talassemia, http://www.fondazionegiambrone.it/

Associazione Ligure Talassemici
Associazione Lotta alla Talassemia di Ferrara,
http://www.altferrara.it/
Associazione Talassemici Torino, http://www.talassemicitorino.it/
Nuova Associaz. Talassemici Italiani

**Jordan**
Jordanian Thalassaemia & Hemophilia Society

**Lebanon**
Chronic Care Center, http://www.chroniccare.org.lb/

**Luxembourg**
Etudier Comb. les Maladies de L'haemoglobin

**Malaysia**
Federation of Malaysian Thalassaemia Societies
Johor Thalassaemia Society
Persatuan Thalassaemia Malaysia
Pulau Penang Thalassemia Society, http://www.penthal.org/

**Maldives**
Society for Health Education, http://www.she.org.mv/

**Malta**
Thalassaemia Awareness Maltese Association

**Morocco**
Thalassaemia-Haemoglobin Diseases Association

**Nepal**
Nepal Thalassaemia Society
**Netherlands**
OSCAR Netherlands, http://www.thalassemie.nl/

**Pakistan**
Pakistan Thalassaemia Welfare Society

Thalassaemia Society of Pakistan, http://www.thalassaemia.org.pk/
Abbotonians Medical Association, http://www.ama.org.pk/
Kashif Iqbal Thalassaemia Care Centre
Pakistan Blood Transfusion Services
Thalassaemia Federation of Pakistan, http://www.tfp.org.pk/
Thalassaemia Patients & Parents Society of Pakistan
Thalassaemia Free Pakistan, http://thalassemia.com.pk/

**Palestine**
Palestine Avenir Foundation
Thalassaemia Patients' Friends Society TPFS

**Philippines**
Mindanao Thalassaemia Foundation, Inc.

**Portugal**
Associacao Portuguesa de Pais e Doentes com Hemoglobinopatias, http://www.appdh.org.pt/

**Romania**
Asociata Persoanelor cu Thalasemie Majora, http://www.thalasemia.ro/thalasemie.html

**Singapore**
Club Rainbow Thal. Major Support Group, http://www.clubrainbow.org/
Thalassemia Society (Singapore), http://www.thalsociety.org/

**South Africa**
South African Thalassaemia Association, http://www.thal.org.za/

**Spain**
Spanish Thalassaemia Association
(ALHETA), http://www.alheta.com/

**Sri Lanka**
Kurunegala Thalassaemia Association

## Syria
Thalassemia Patients and Hereditary Blood Diseases

## Taiwan
Taiwan Thalassaemia Association, http://tta.bexweb.tw/

## Thailand
Thalassaemia Foundation of Thailand

## Trinidad
Society for Inherited & Severe Blood Disorders

## Tunisia
Alphatt Tunisie

## Turkey
Akdeniz Thalasemi Dernegi
TADAD Thalassaemia Patient Parent Association
Thalassaemia Federation of Turkey,
http://www.talasemi.org/ Foundation of Mediterranean
Blood Disease

## United Arab Emirates
Emirates Thalassaemia Society, http://www.thalassemia.org.ae/
UAE Genetic Diseases Association, http://www.uaegda.ae/
## United Kingdom
North England Bone Marrow & Thalassaemia Association
(NEBATA),
http://www.cmft.nhs.uk/directorates/nebata/nebata.asp
United Kingdom Thalassaemia Society,
http://www.ukts.org/ Oscar Sandwell,
http://www.oscarsandwell.org.uk/

## United States of America
Cooley's Anemia Foundation, http://www.cooleysanemia.org/

## Patient Resources

Thalassaemia Patients and Friends,
http://www.thalassemiapatientsandfriends.com/
Sickle Cell Society, UK,
http://www.sicklecellsociety.org/ Sickle Cell Disease
Association of America,
 http://www.sicklecelldisease.org/
European Patients Forum (EPF), http://www.eu-patient.eu/
International Alliance of Patients' Organizations (IAPO)
http://www.patientsorganizations.org/
Sickle Cell and Thalassemia Patients Network, US,
http://www.sctpn.org/
PatientView, http://www.patient-view.com/
European Organisation for Rare Diseases (EURORDIS),
http://www.eurordis.org/
Blood: The Vital Connection, http://www.hematology.org/patients
International Federation of Blood Donor Organizations,
http://www.fiods.org/
Thalassemia Support BC: The Vancouver Thalassemia society of BC
https://bcthalassemia.ca/

## Medical Resources

HIV information from WHO,
http://www.who.int/topics/hivinfections/en
HIV and Hepatitis, http://www.hivandhepatitis.com/
International Consortium for Blood Safety
(ICBS), http://www.icbs-web.org/
International Society for Blood Transfusion
(ISBT), http://www.isbt-web.org/
Blood safety information from WHO,

http://www.who.int/topics/blood safety/en
ITHANet web portal for thalassaemias and hemoglobinopathies,
http://www.ithanet.eu/
European Genetics Foundation,
http://www.eurogene.org/portale/index.php
American Society of Hematology–Find a Hematologist,
http://www.talassemiaricerca.it/
THAL-Lab, Italy,
http://www.talassemiaricerca.unife.it/ European and
International Organizations
European Medicines Agency (EMEA),
http://www.emea.europa.eu/
US Food and Drug Administration (FDA),
http://www.fda.gov/Drugs/default.htm
European Public Health Alliance (EPHA), http://www.epha.org/
European Platform for Patients' Organisations, Science and
Industry
(EPPOSI), http://www.epposi.org/
EU Executive Agency for Health and Consumers (EAHC),
http://ec.europa.eu/eahc/
European Organisation for Rare Diseases (EURORDIS),
http://www.eurordis.org/
Drug Information Association (DIA),
http://www.diahome.org/DIAHome
EU Rare Diseases Task Force, http://www.rdtf.org/
Cure2Children Foundation, http://www.cure2children.org/

# World Health Organization (WHO)

WHO main site, http://www.who.int/
Noncommunicable diseases,
http://www.who.int/topics/chronicdiseases/en/
Global Collaboration on Blood Safety (GCBS),
http://www.who.int/bloodsafety/gcbs/mission/en

## WHO Regional Offices

Africa, http://www.afro.who.int/
Americas, http://www.paho.org/
South East Asia,
http://www.searo.who.int/ Europe,
http://www.euro.who.int/
Eastern Mediterranean,
http://www.emro.who.int/ Western Pacific,
http://www.wpro.who.int/

# About the Author

Born in Calabria, Italy, and immigrated to Canada at age twelve — the eighth of nine children. Married for forty-five years to Pasquale Sammarco, and mother of two children. Held a career in the insurance industry for twenty years as an Accredited General Insurance Broker.

Founder and president of the Vancouver Thalassemia Society of British Columbia. Past president of a woman's lodge in the Italian community, doing volunteer work for the Vancouver community, and board member of the Lower Mainland Grief Recovery Society. Serafina cherishes family and good friends and loves to engage in intellectual and meaningful conversations.

Loves to dance with husband Pasquale and special group of friends. Enjoys long walks in nature to help clear the mind and restore the soul.

Contact information: Serafina Sammarco
serafina@sammarco.ca | http://www.sammarco.ca

# Isabella Marie Sammarco

(Oct. 7th, 1971 – July 29th, 1986)

Isabella was known by her family and friends for her tremendous zest and respect for life; with a sparkle in her eyes and a contagious smile, she taught those around her to appreciate their lives and to love one another.

Although she was very much aware from an early age that her life would be short, this knowledge did not stop her from living with a purpose and making each day count.

Isabella was diagnosed at eight months with Thalassemia Major – a genetic blood disorder – that required her to have regular, monthly transfusions to survive.

She fought vigorously to overcome the numerous obstacles that she encountered during her brief life until her small body could fight no more. Isabella died two months short of her fifteenth birthday. This book is the heartfelt, truthful account of a brave soul and her dedicated family. It is a story that will touch all who read it and inspire those looking for guidance and hope.

www.ingramcontent.com/pod-product-compliance
Lightning Source LLC
Chambersburg PA
CBHW021648120626
46545CB00002B/751